ISBN 978-1-333-68205-7
PIBN 10535106

# 1 MONTH OF
# FREE
# READING

## at

## www.ForgottenBooks.com

By purchasing this book you are eligible for one month membership to ForgottenBooks.com, giving you unlimited access to our entire collection of over 700,000 titles via our web site and mobile apps.

To claim your free month visit:
www.forgottenbooks.com/free535106

English
Français
Deutsche
Italiano
Español
Português

# www.forgottenbooks.com

**Mythology** Photography **Fiction**
Fishing Christianity **Art** Cooking
Essays Buddhism Freemasonry
Medicine **Biology** Music **Ancient**
**Egypt** Evolution Carpentry Physics
Dance Geology **Mathematics** Fitness
Shakespeare **Folklore** Yoga Marketing
**Confidence** Immortality Biographies
Poetry **Psychology** Witchcraft
Electronics Chemistry History **Law**
Accounting **Philosophy** Anthropology
Alchemy Drama Quantum Mechanics
Atheism Sexual Health **Ancient History**
**Entrepreneurship** Languages Sport
Paleontology Needlework Islam
**Metaphysics** Investment Archaeology
Parenting Statistics Criminology
**Motivational**

# GLICKSTEIN'S SYSTEM

## LADIES', MISSES' AND CHILDREN'S ❦ GARMENTS ❦

## PRACTICAL METHODS OF DESIGNING ACCORDING TO PROPORTIONS.

### By PH. GLICKSTEIN.

### 1909.

The Reich Printing Co., 167 Rivington Street,
NEW YORK.

# DIPLOMA

## Ph. Glickstein's Designing School

### This Certifies that

*Max Goldberg*

Has completed the Course of Instruction in

*Designing, Grading, Sketching, and Fitting of Ladies' Garments,*

Prescribed in **The Glickstein Designing School**

and has passed a satisfactory examination and is therefore declared to be a graduate of said Institution.

In Testimony Whereof I have hereunto affixed my hand in the City of New York, this *Twenty-second* day of *Jan 1909*

*Ph. Glickstein*

Reduced reproduction of diploma awarded
to each student.

*Philip Glickstein.*

# Preface.

---

¶ The numerous years of constant personal contact with my pupils; the close and studious observations I made of their requisites; the various and diverse inquiries by them made; the many years that I devoted, both, as designer and instructor; each and all of these facts have prompted and enabled me to produce this volume.

¶ The vast amount of experience gained has taught me to formulate this publication in a manner most comprehensive to my pupils. That this book shall be both an aid and a guide to those that make themselves familiar with its contents is my aim.

¶ It is with these sincere motives in view that the following work is presented to the public.

PHILIP GLICKSTEIN

Author.


New York, July, 1909.

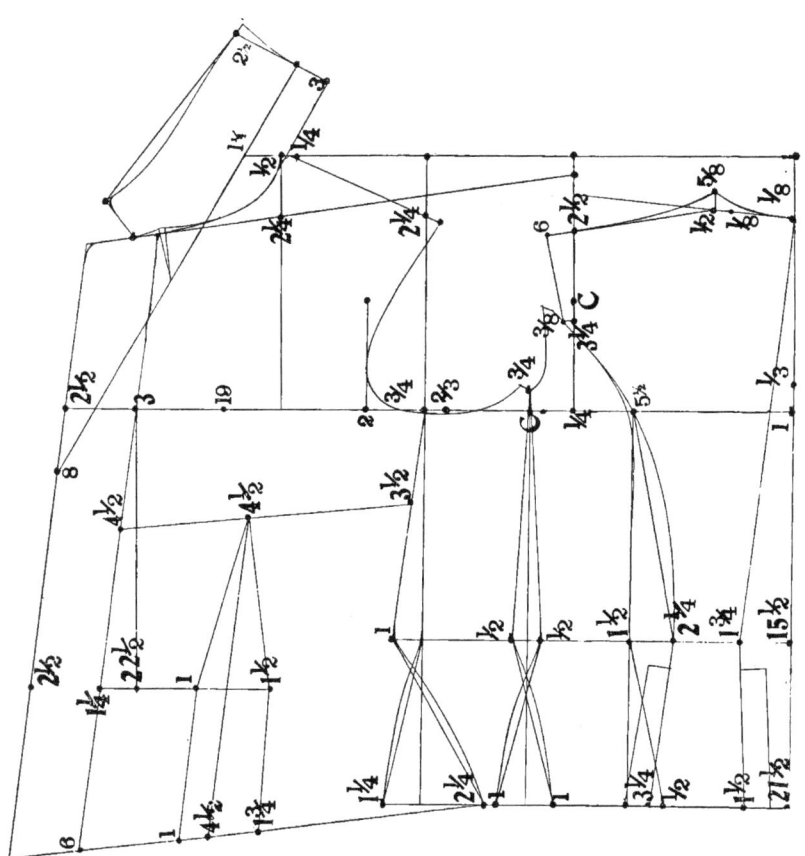

# DIAGRAM No 1.

Fly front tight fitting Jacket.

פלאי פראנט טייט פיטטינג דזשעקעט.

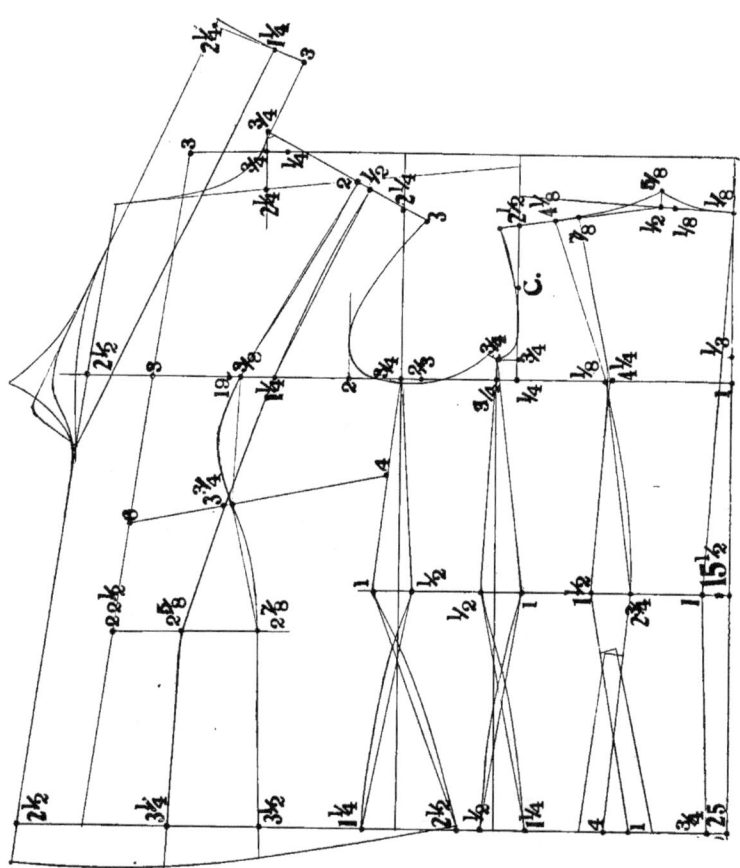

## DIAGRAM No. 2.

French tight fitting Jacket in 10 gores with shawl collar

פרענטש טייט פיטטינג דזשעקעט אין 10 גארם מיט א שאהל קאללער.

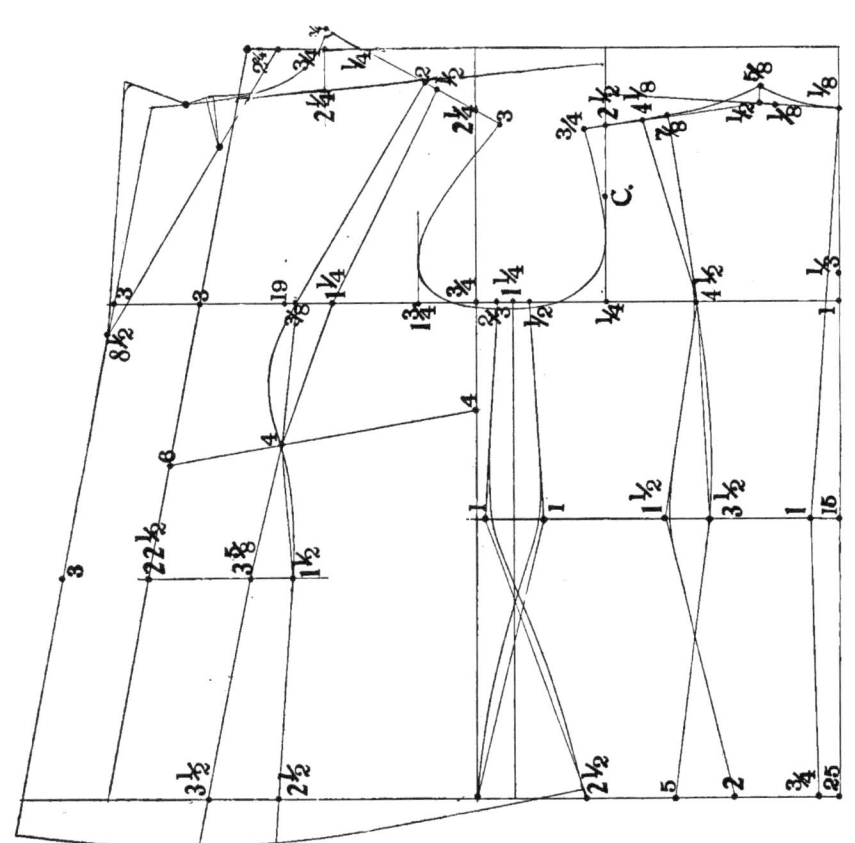

# DIAGRAM No. 3.

## Hipless Jacket in 8 Gores.

דזשעקעט אָהנע היפס אין 8 גאָרס.

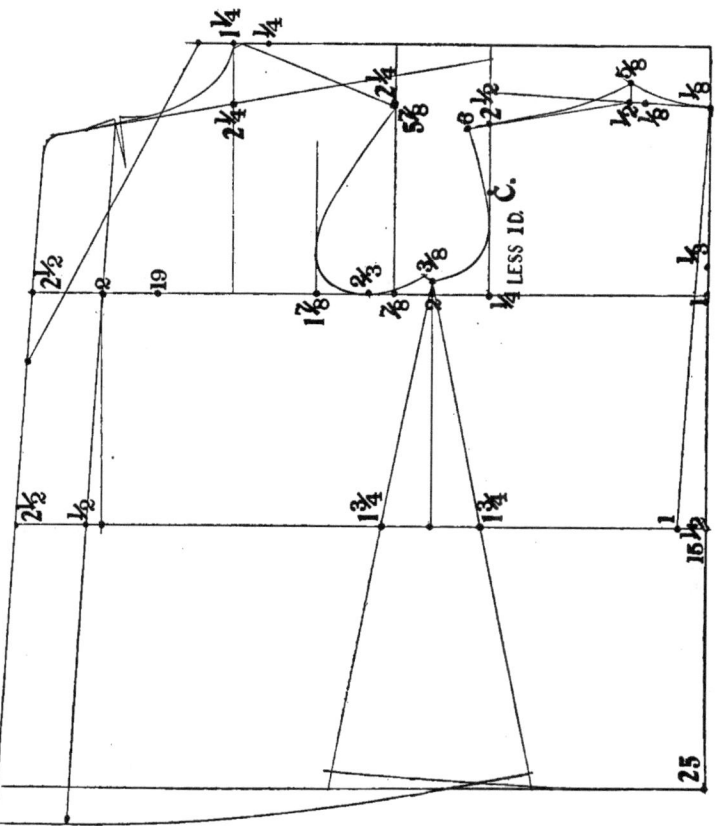

## DIAGRAM No. 9.

Box Coat. באם קאוט.

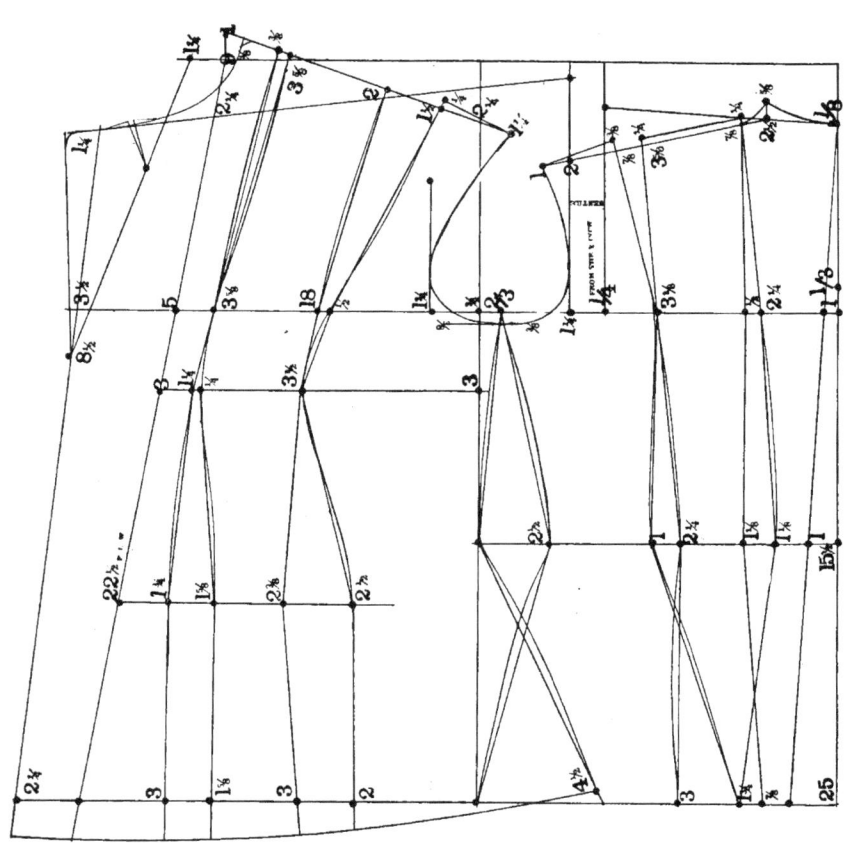

## DIAGRAM No. 5.

Tight fitting Jacket in 11 gores.  Full back.

טייט פיטטינג דזשעקעט אין 11 גאָרס.  פּוללער בעק.

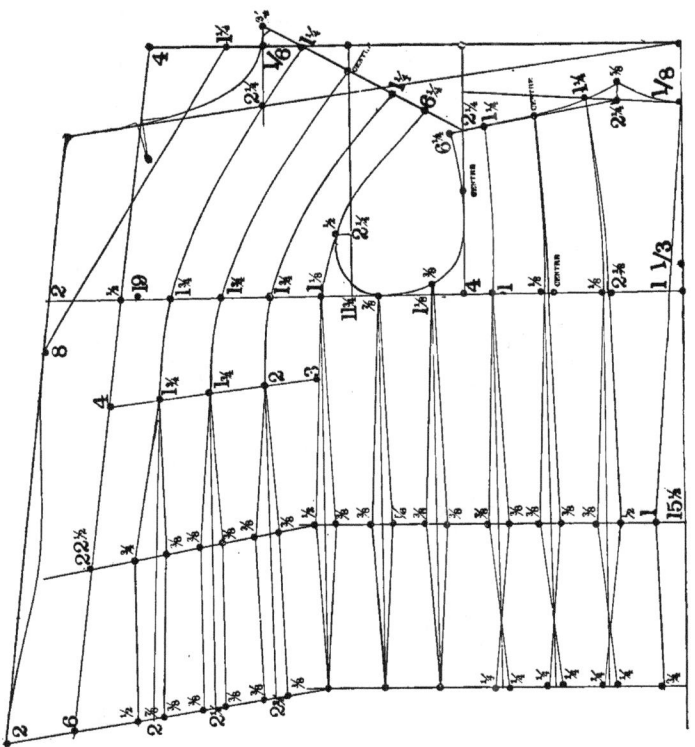

**DIAGRAM No. 6.**

Corset jacket. This jacket has no allowance for seams

קאָרסעט דזשעקעט. עס ערלויבט קיינע סיעמס.

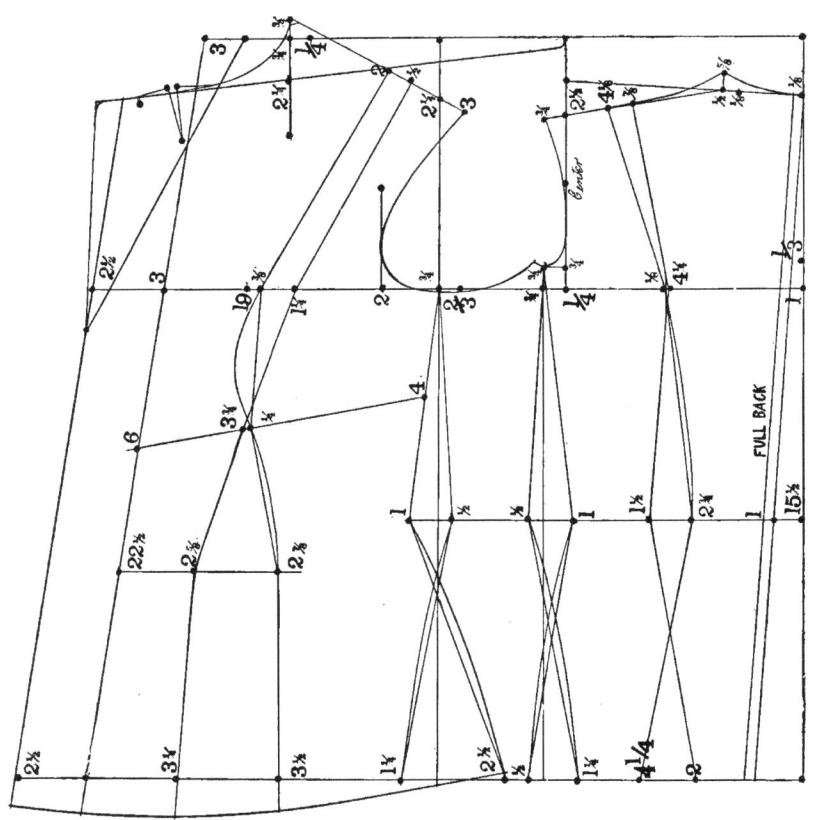

## DIAGRAM No. 7.

French tight fitting jacket with full back.

פרענטש טייט פיטטינג דזשעקעט מיט א פאָללען בעק.

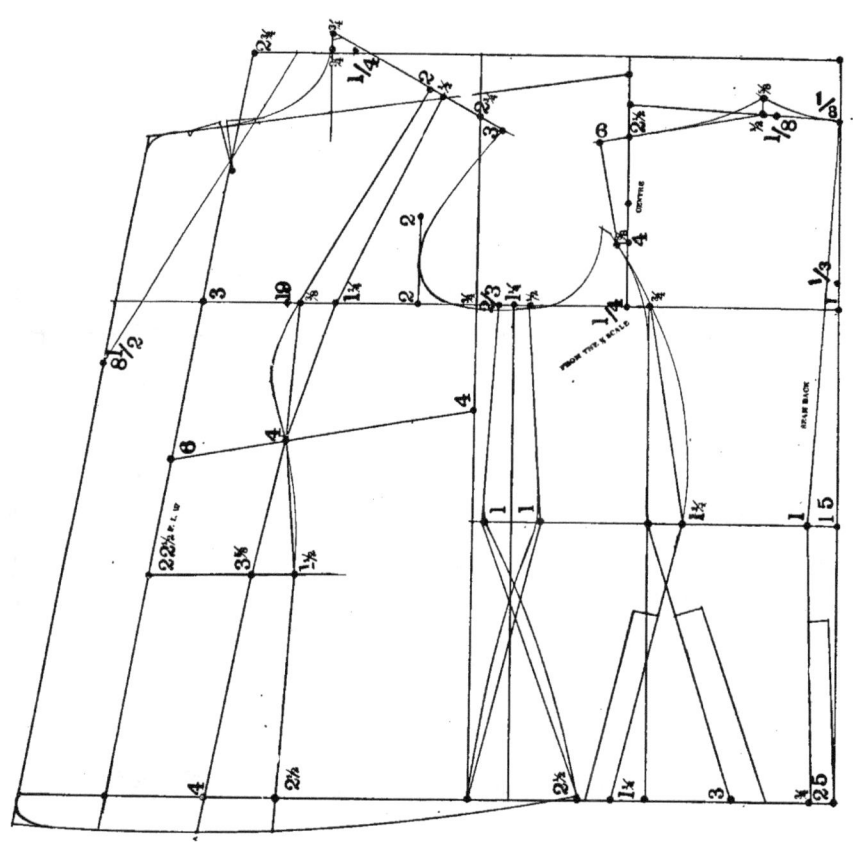

## DIAGRAM No. 8.

### Hipless coat in 8 parts. French front.

היפלעס קאוט אין 8 טהיילען.   פרענטש פראָנט.

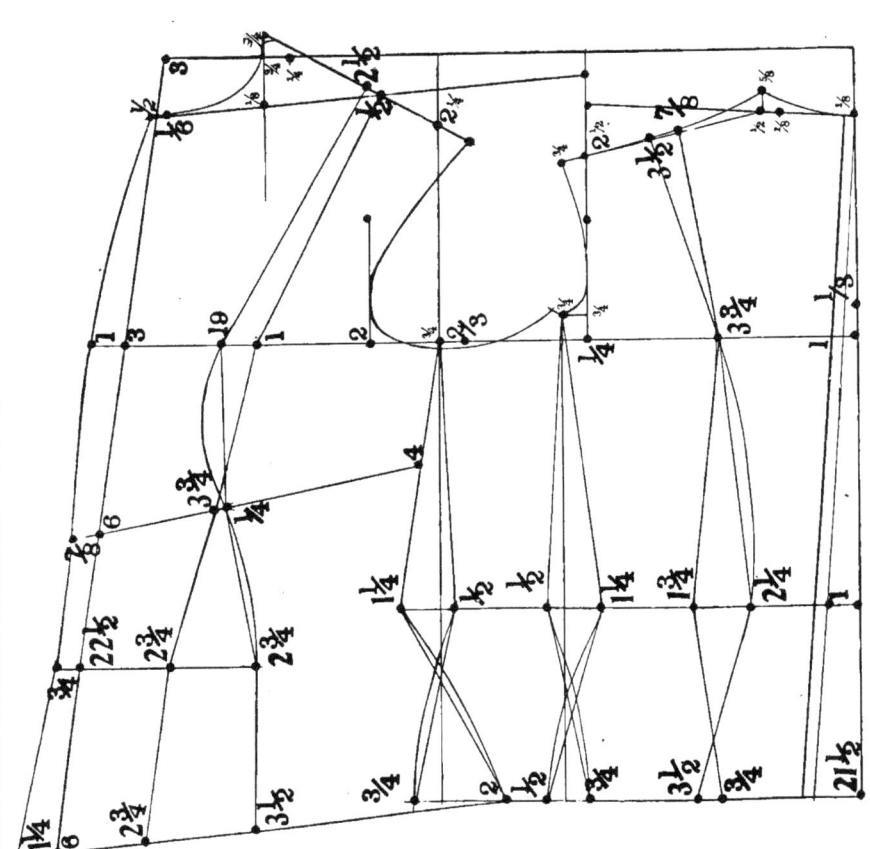

## DIAGRAM No 9.

Short tight fitting military coat with full back.

קורצער טייט פיטטינג מיליטארי קאוט מיט א פולען בעק.

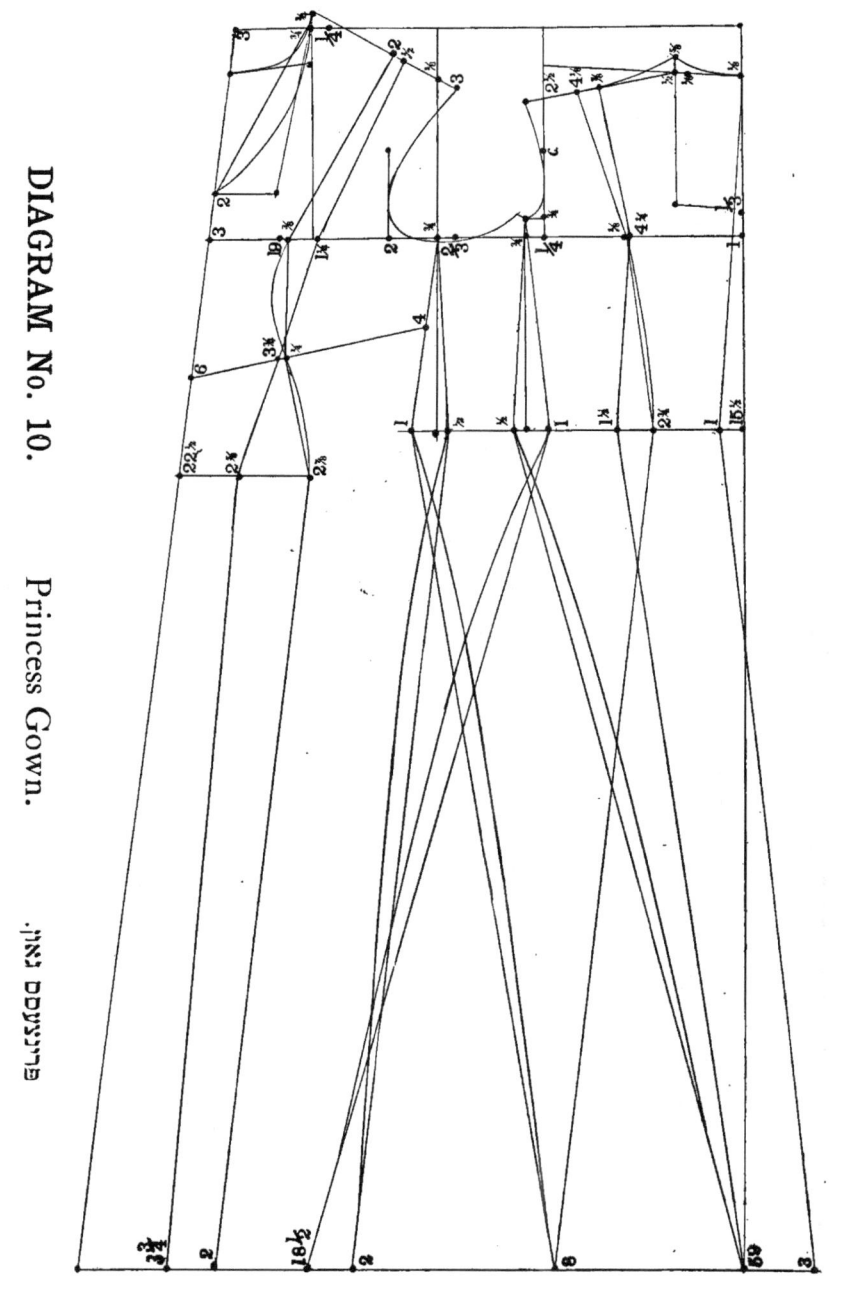

DIAGRAM No. 10.

Princess Gown.

גליקסטיינס סיסטעם.

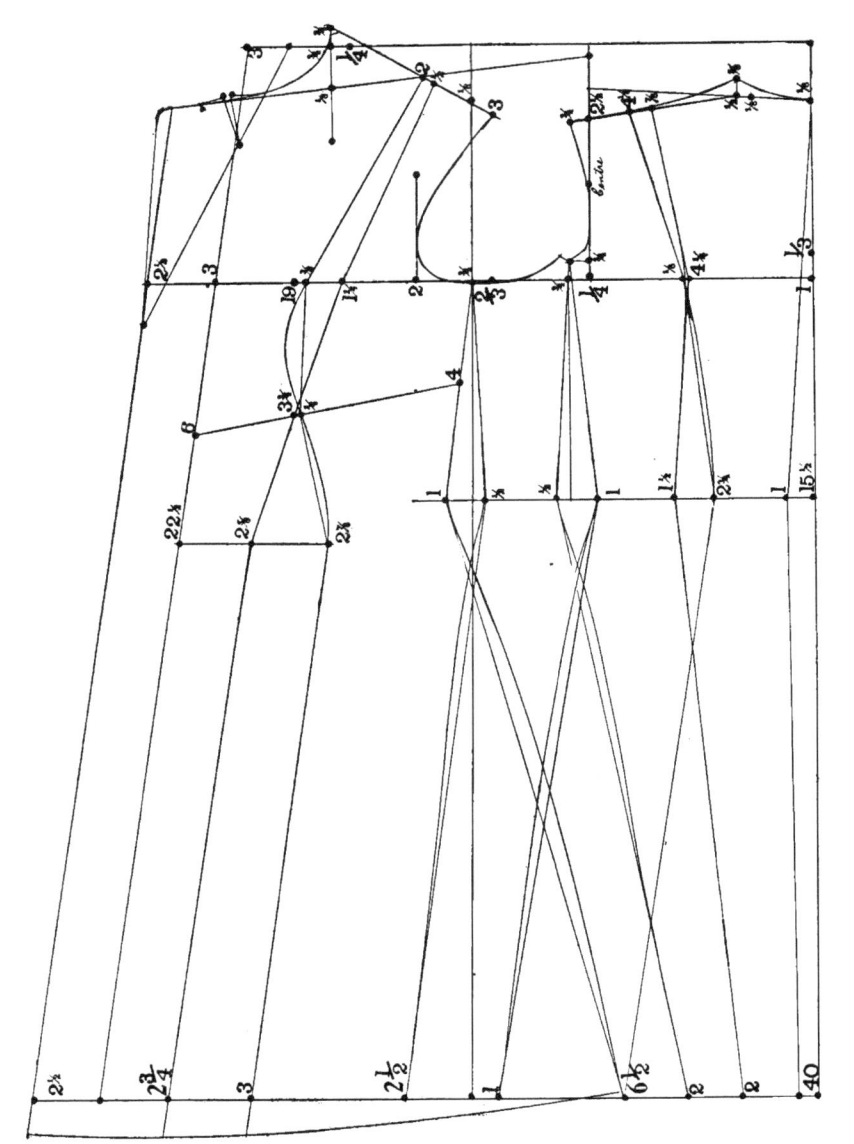

**DIAGRAM No. 11.**

Long, tight fitting coat.

לאננער, טייט פיטטינג קאוט,

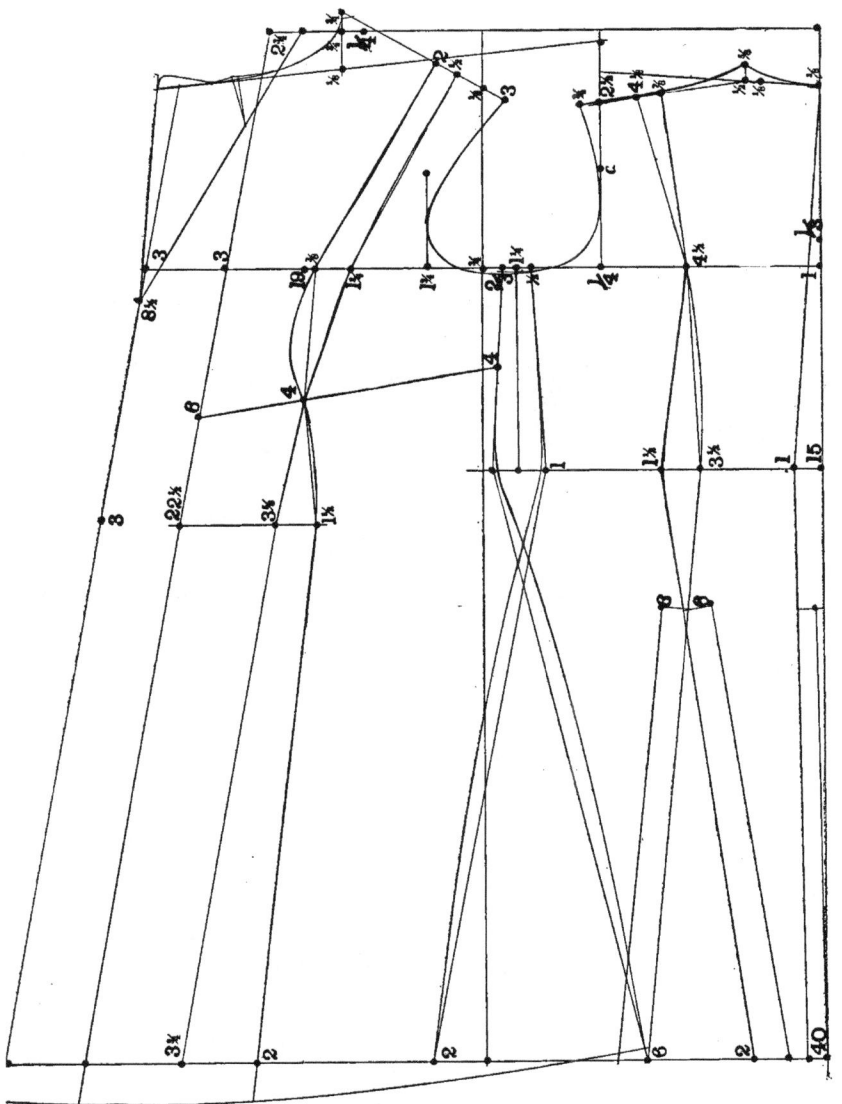

## DIAGRAM No. 12.

Long, hipless coat.

לאנגער קאוט אהנע היפס.

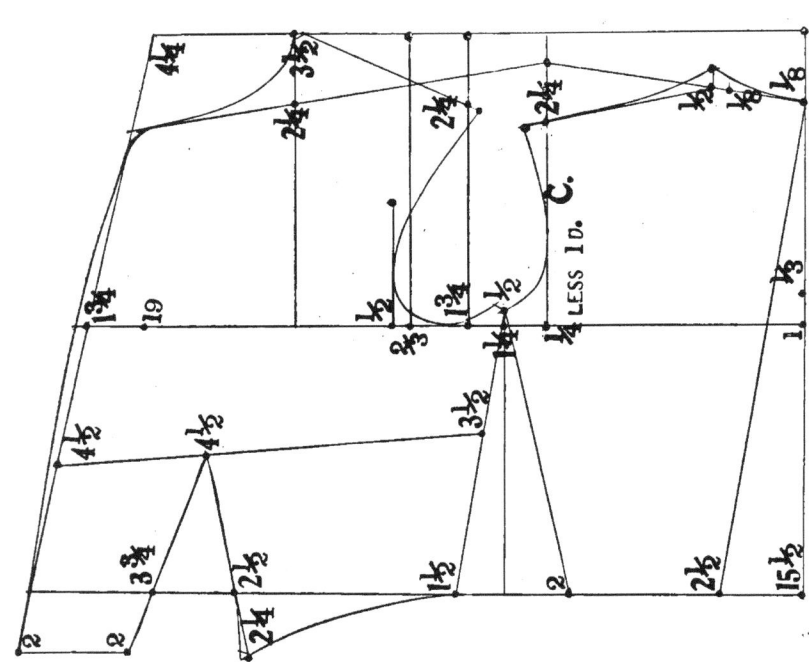

## DIAGRAM No. 13.

Eaton  Jacket.                איטאן דזשעקעט.

**DIAGRAM No. 14.**

Russian Blouse. רוססישע בלויזע.

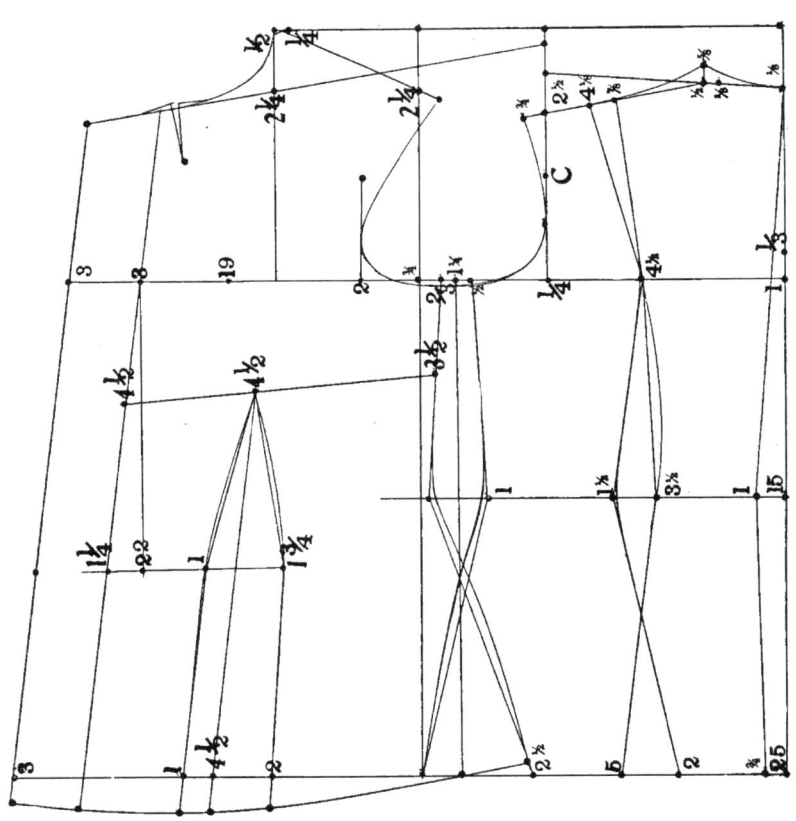

## DIAGRAM No. 15.

Hipless coat with french back and 1 dott in the front

קאוט אָהנע היפס מיט א פרענטש בעק און 1 דאָט אין פראָנט.

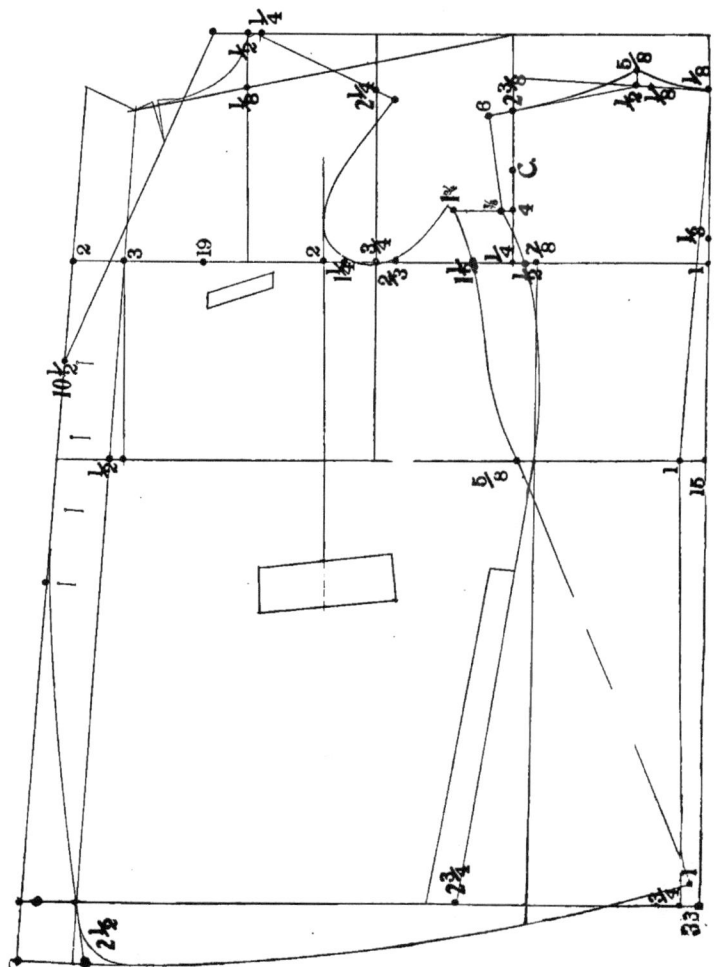

# DIAGRAM No. 16.

Long coat in 4 parts.

לאנגער קאוט אין 4 טהיילען.

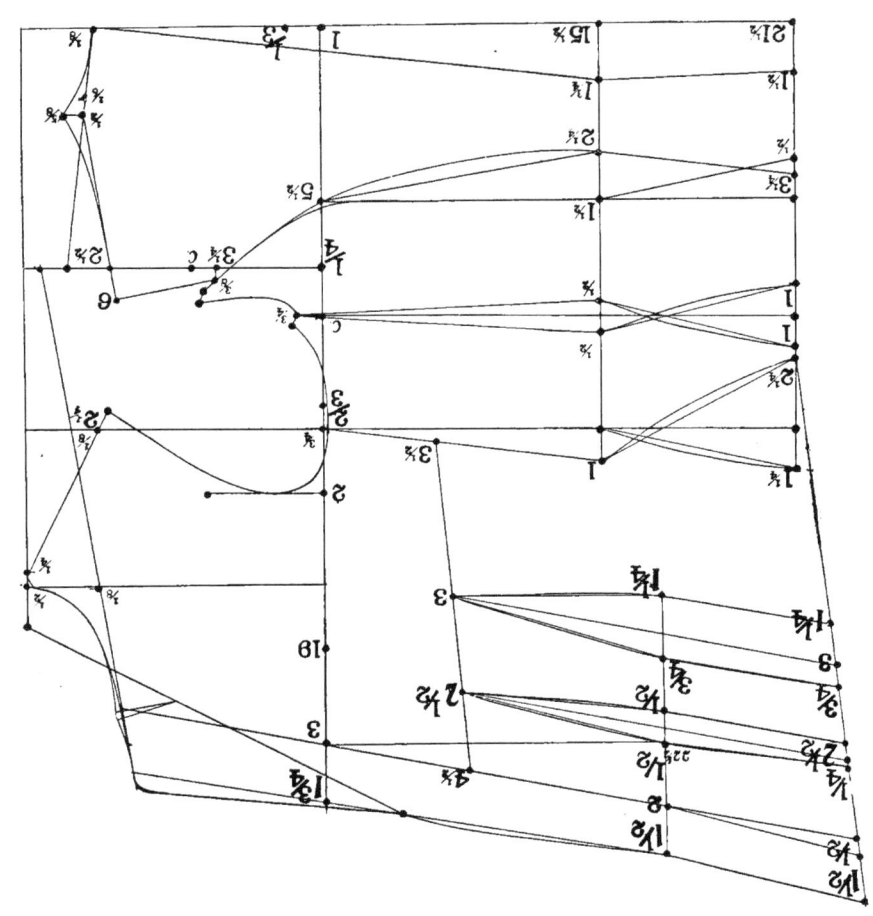

# DIAGRAM No. 17.

Tight fitting Jacket with 2 dots in the front.

טייט פיטטינג דזשעקעט מיט 2 דאטס אין פראָנט.

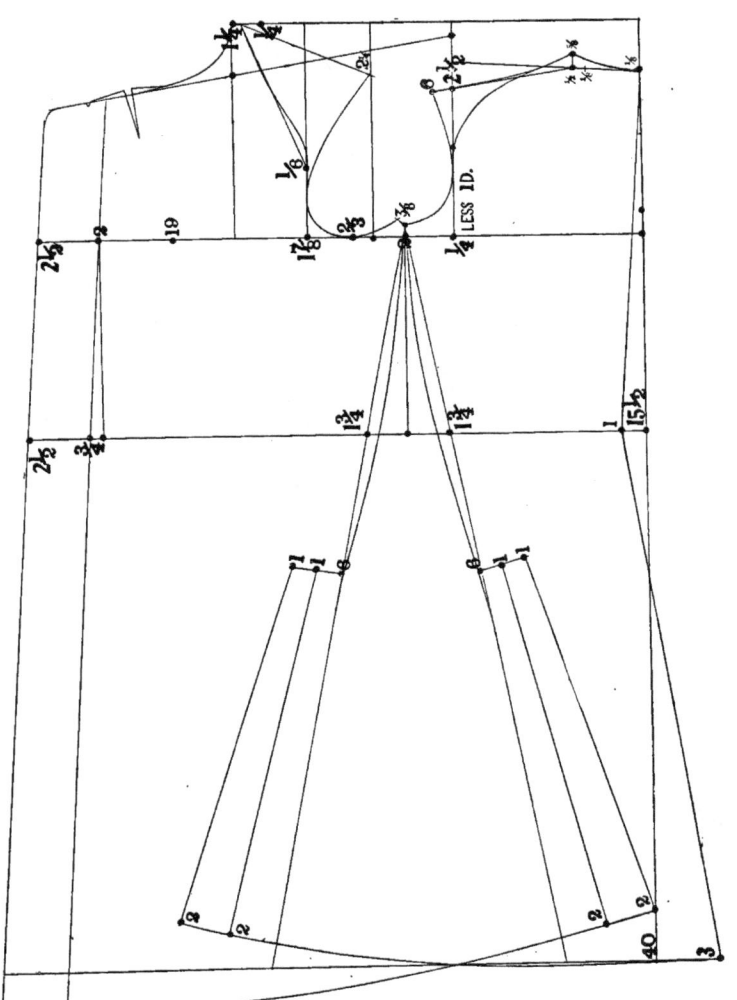

## DIAGRAM No. 18.

Ragalan. רעגאלען.

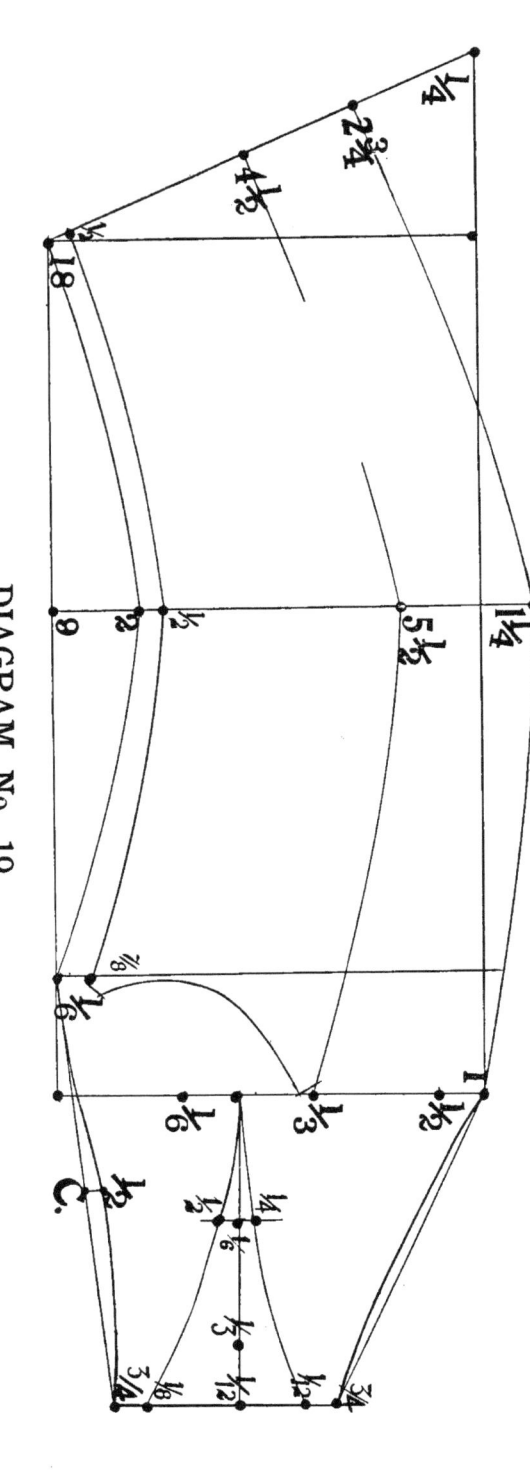

**DIAGRAM No. 19.**

Ragalan Sleeve

ראגלאן סליוו

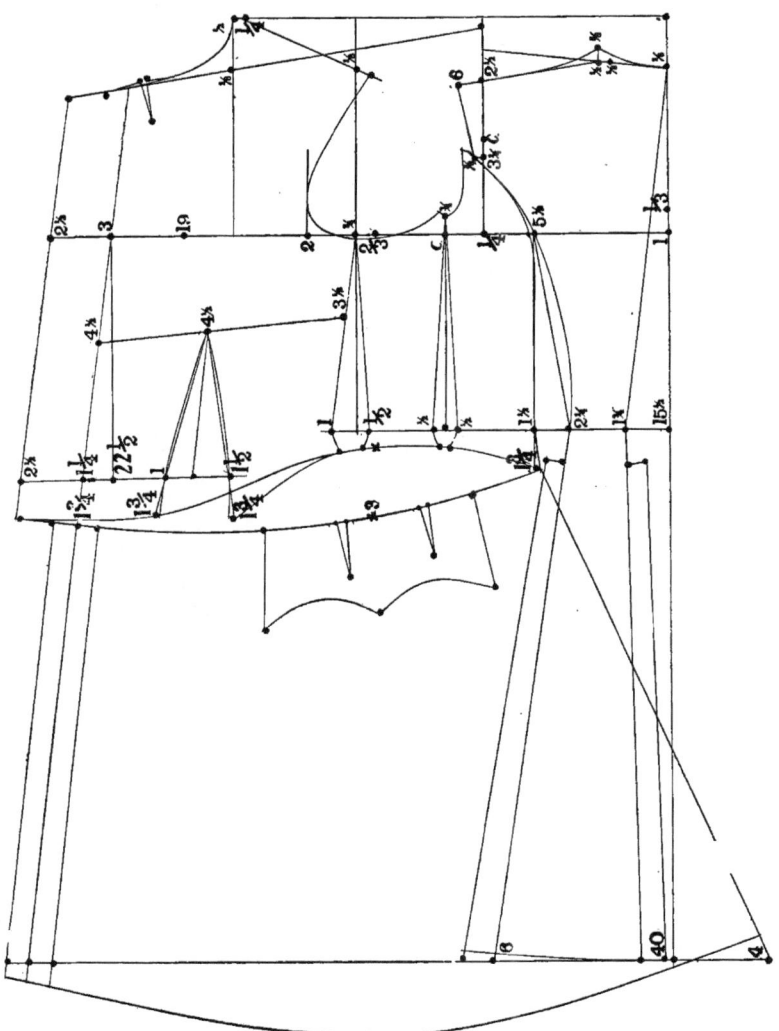

**DIAGRAM No. 20.**

Ladies' Prince Albert.

לײדיעס׳ פרינס אלבערט.

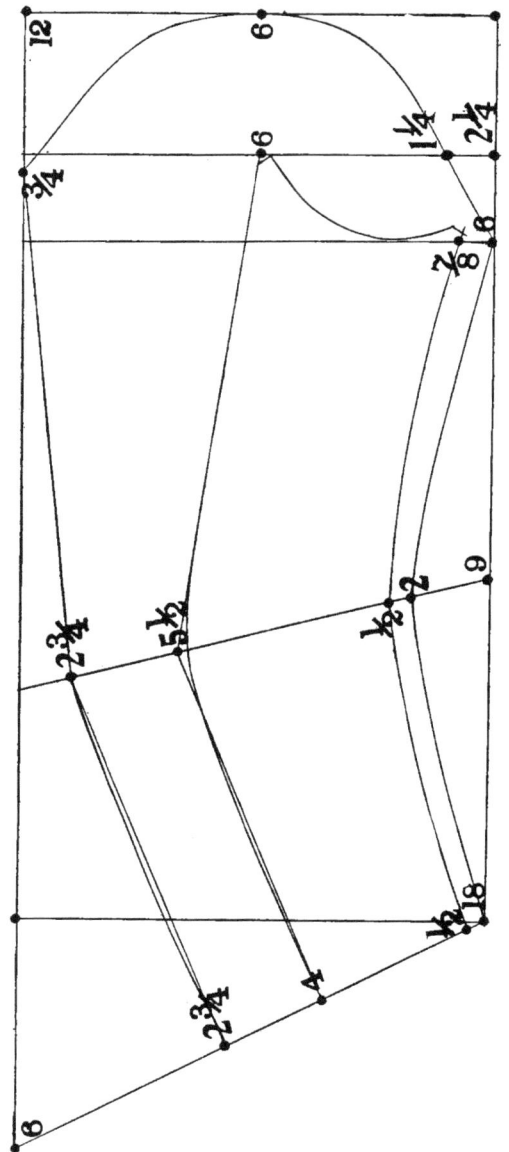

# DIAGRAM No. 21.

Narrow Coat Sleeve.     שמאָלער קאָט סליוו.

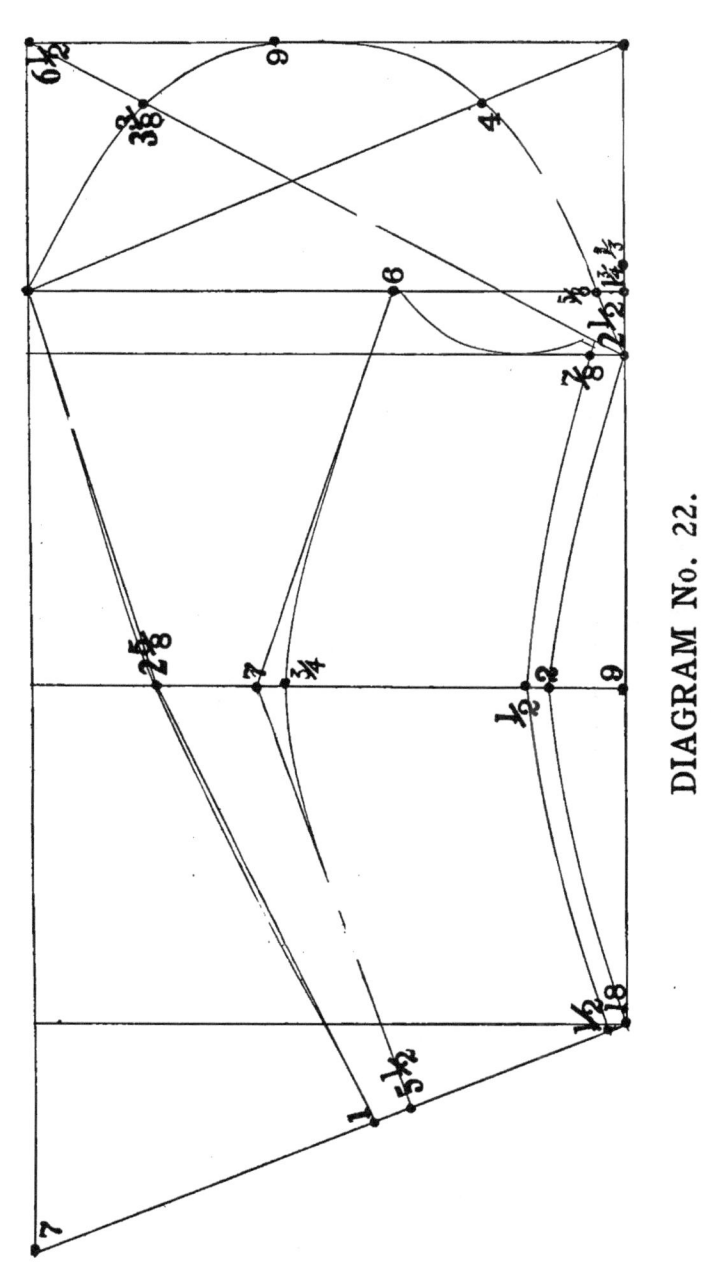

**DIAGRAM No. 22.**

Sleeve with wide top or head.    סליוו מיט א וויידען טאפ אדער העד.

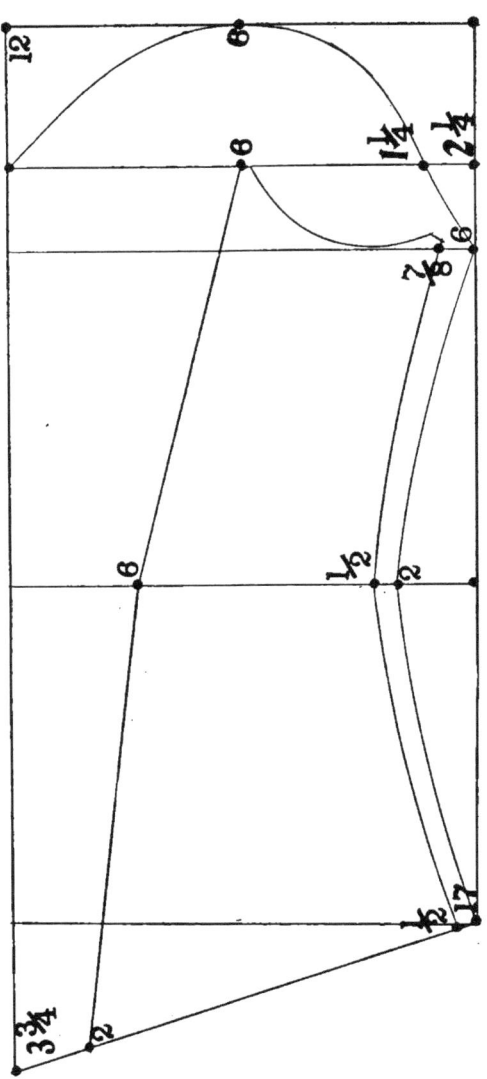

## DIAGRAM No 23.

Bishop Sleeve.

ביישאפ סליוו.

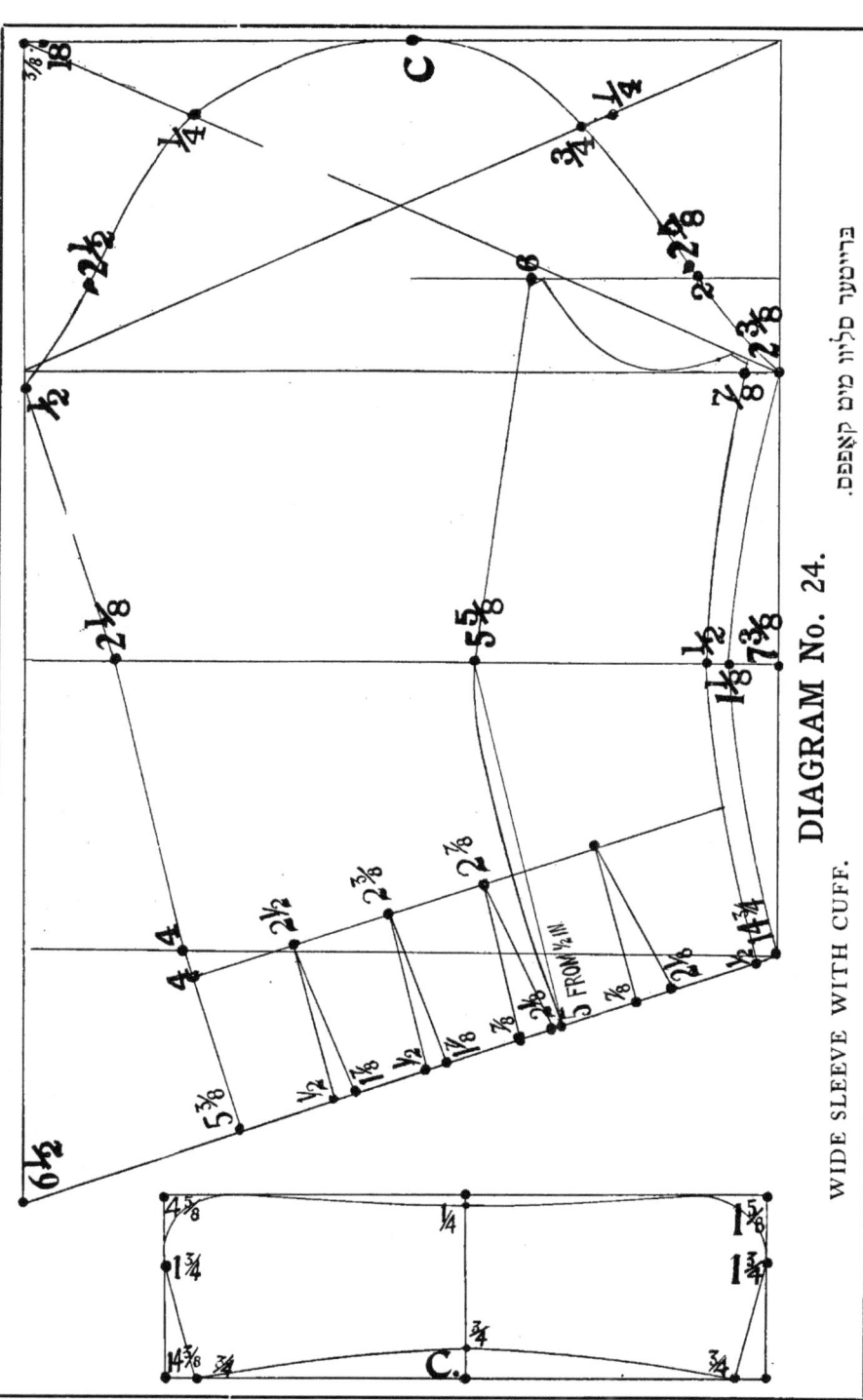

DIAGRAM No. 24.

WIDE SLEEVE WITH CUFF.

פאטערן פיר ווייטע קופף.

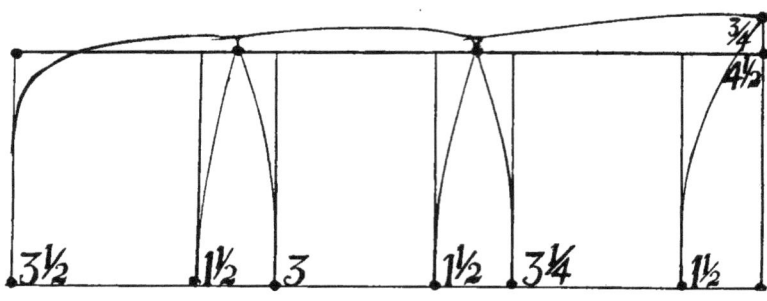

### DIAGRAM No. 25.

Storm collar in 6 pieces.     סטאָרם קאָללער אין 6 טהיילען,

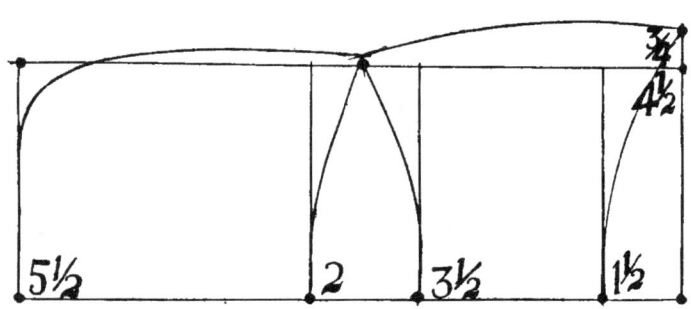

### DIAGRAM No 26.

Storm collar in 4 pieces.     סטאָרם קאָללער אין 4 טהיילען.

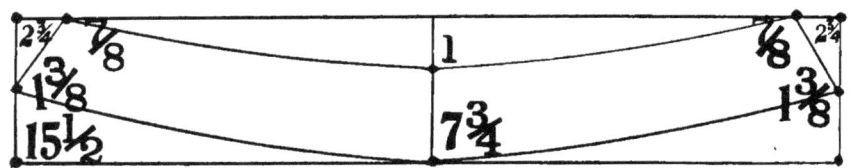

### DIAGRAM No. 27.

Standing collar.     שטעהענדינגער קאָללער.

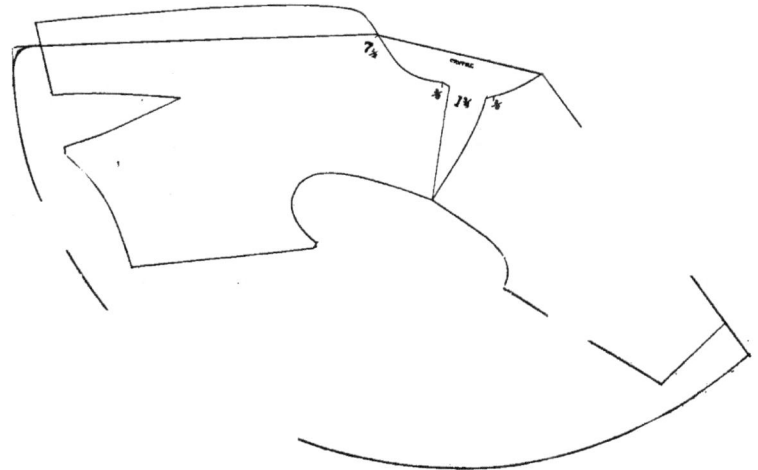

## DIAGRAM No. 28.

### Cape with a Dot.

קעיפ מיט א דאט.

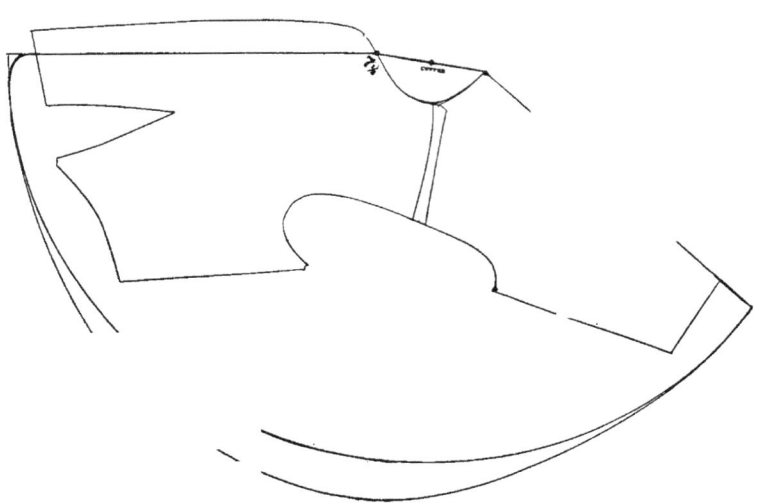

## DIAGRAM No. 29.

Cape without a dot. קעיפ אהנע דאט.

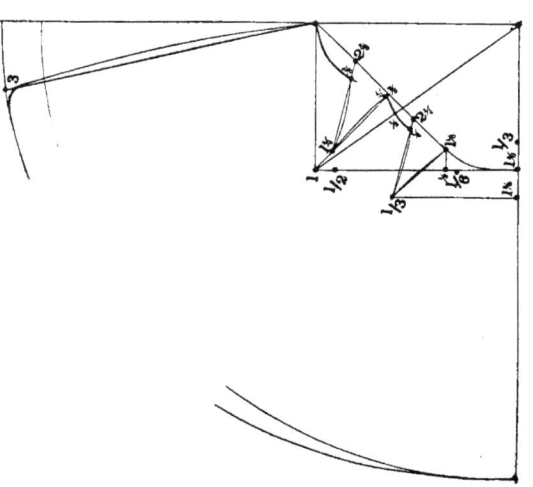

## DIAGRAM No. 30.

System for a cape. סיסטעם פיר א קעיפ.

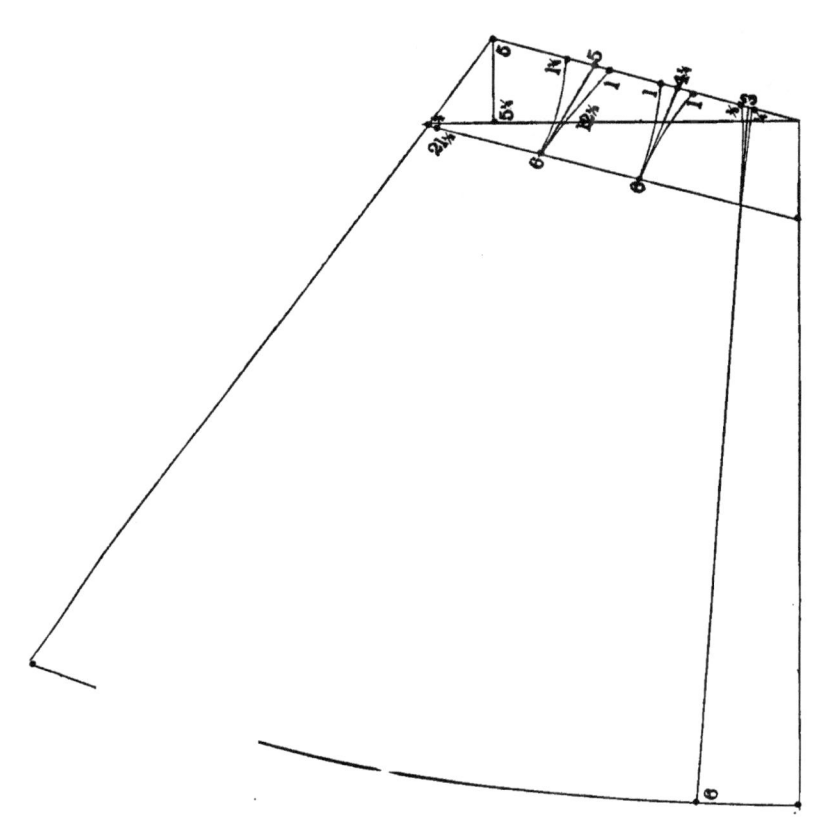

# DIAGRAM No. 31.

## Three Gore Skirt.    .סקווירט אין 3 גארס.

### MEASURMENTS.

Waist, 25,    Front Length, 41,    Hips, 43,
Side Length, 44,    Back Length, 46.

The same measurements apply to all the skirts.

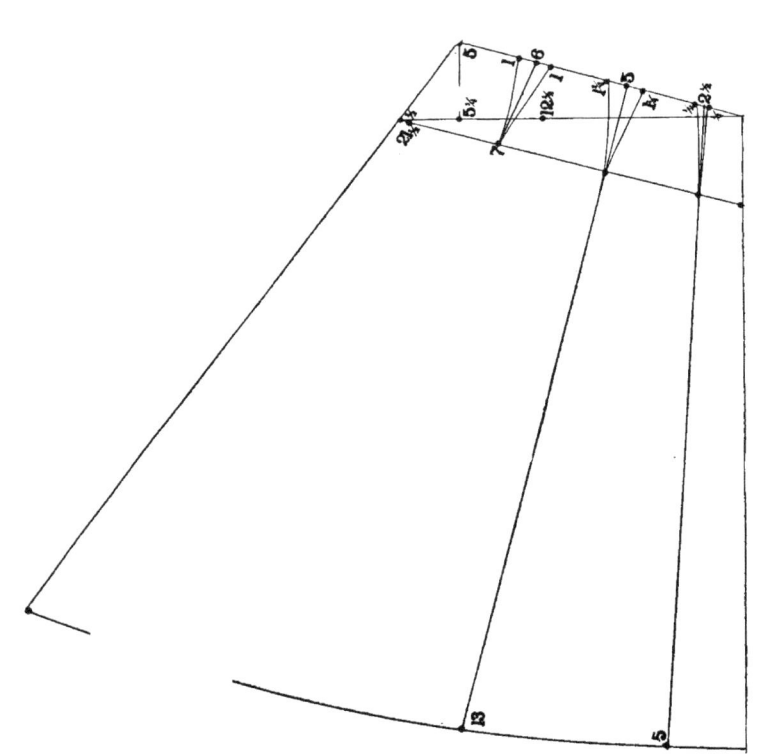

# DIAGRAM No. 32.

## Five Gore Skirt.

סקווירט אין 5 גארם.

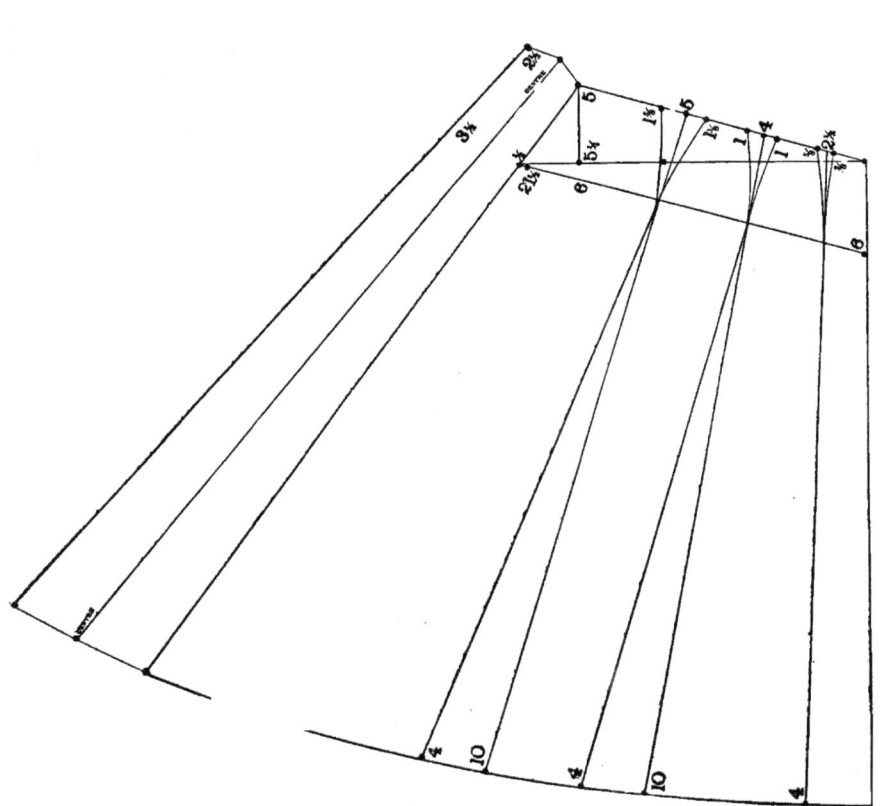

# DIAGRAM No. 33.

## Seven Gore Skirt.

סקוירט אין 7 גארס.

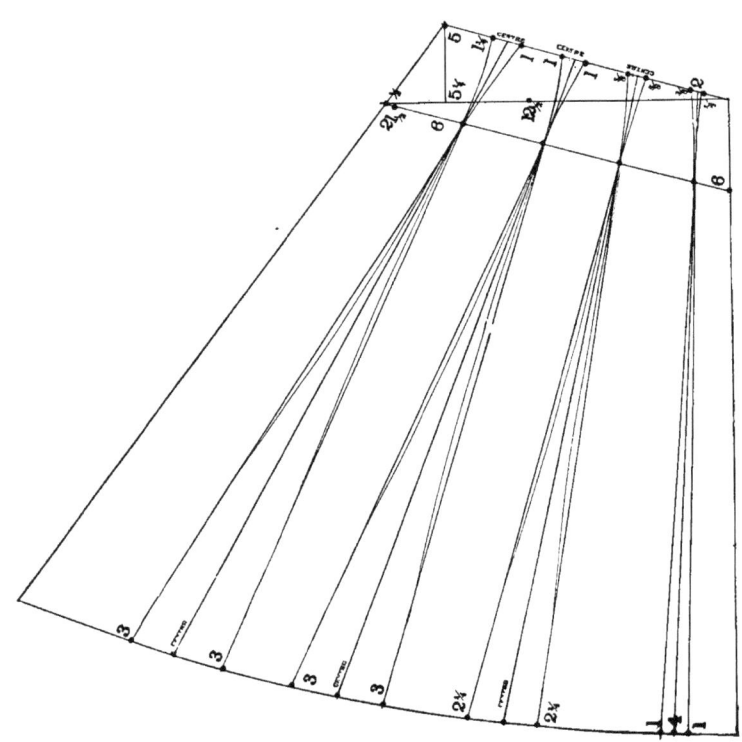

## DIAGRAM No. 34.

### Nine Gore Skirt.

סקוירט אין 9 גאָרס.

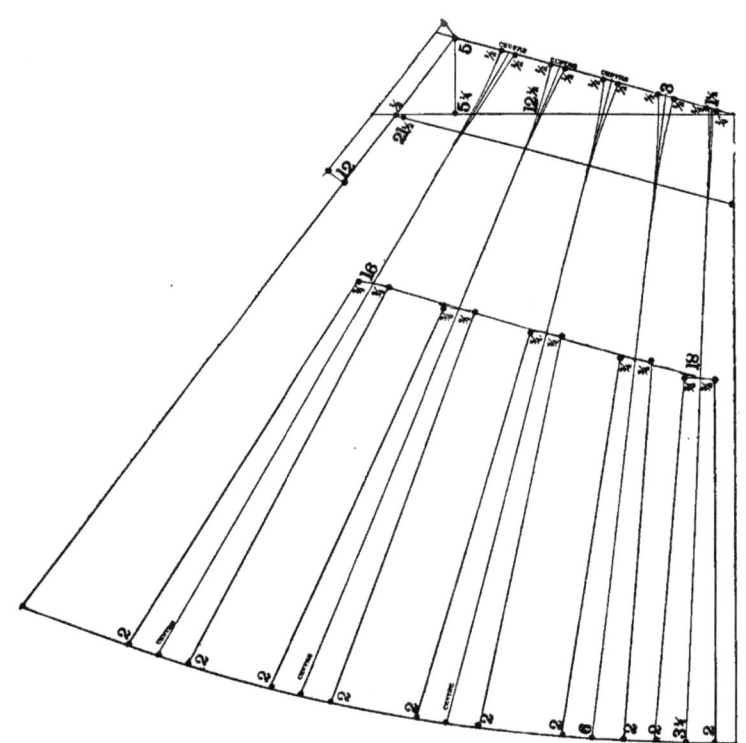

## DIAGRAM No. 35.

### Eleven Gore Skirt.

סקווירט אין 11 נארס.

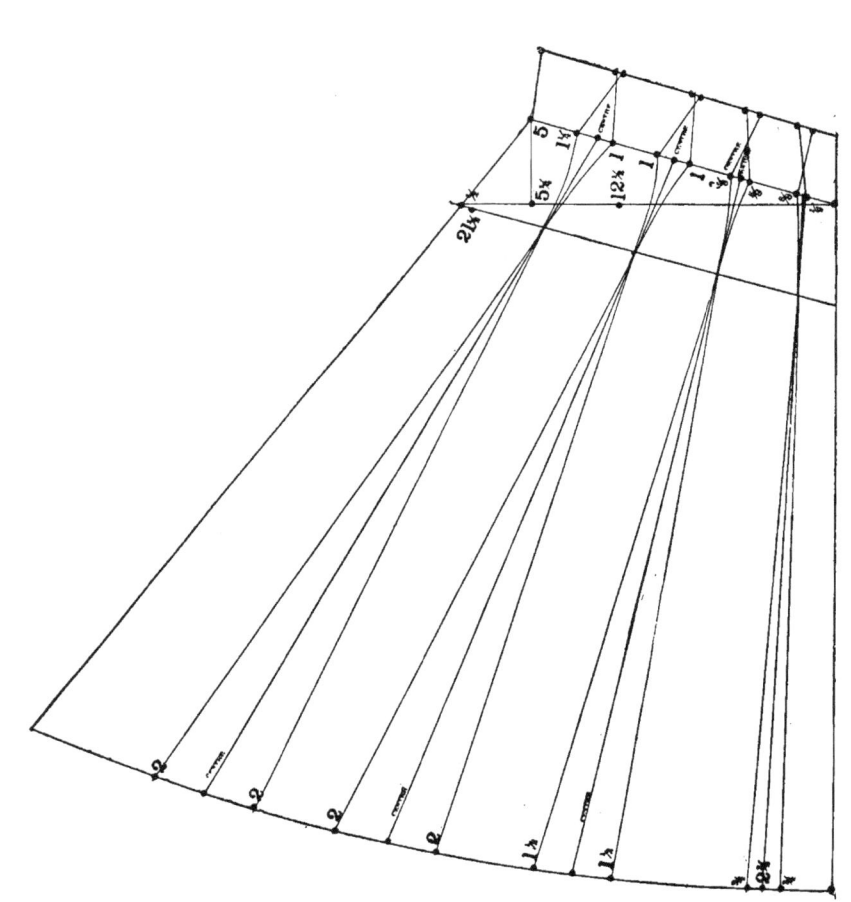

## DIAGRAM No. 36.

### Nine Gore Corset Skirt.

קאָרסעט סקווירט אין 9 גאָרס.

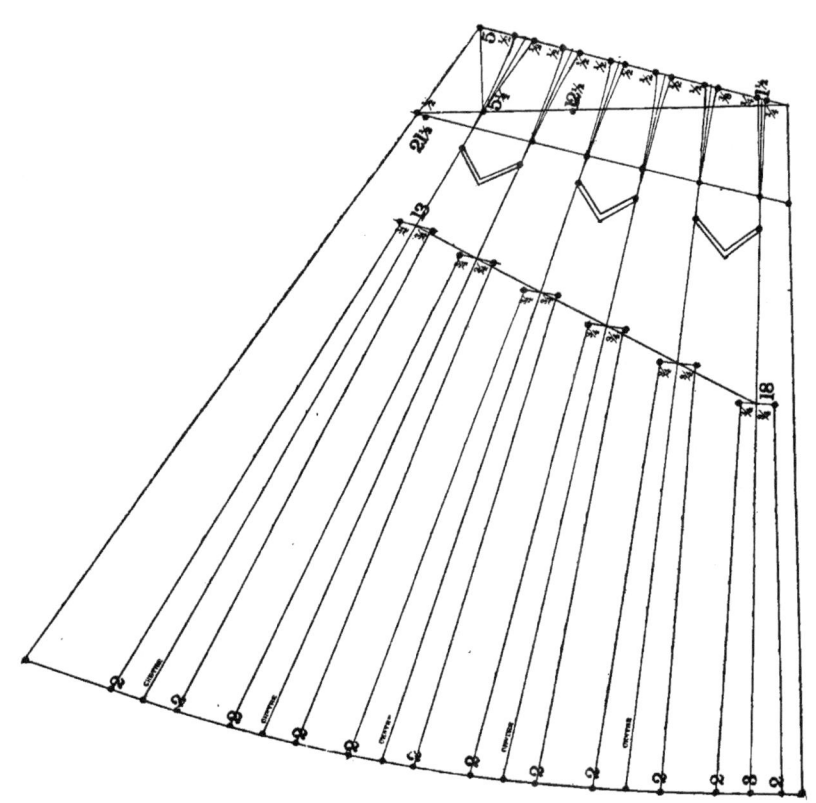

**DIAGRAM No. 37.**

Thirteen Gore Skirt.

סקוירט אין 13 גאָרס.

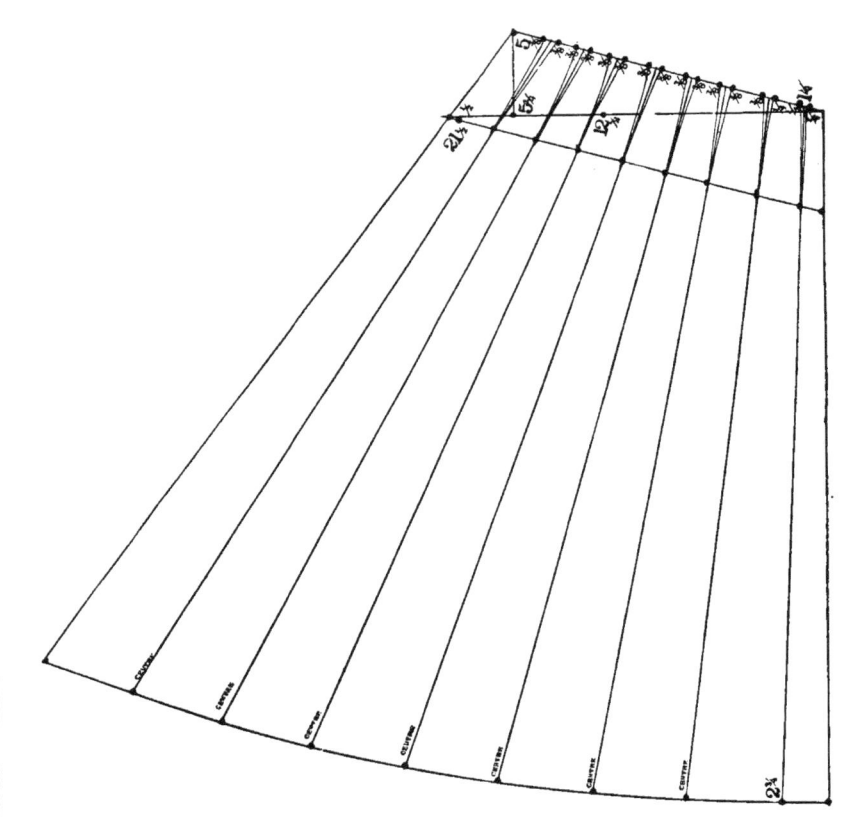

## DIAGRAM No. 38.

### Seventeen Gore Skirt.

סקווירט אין 17 גאָרס.

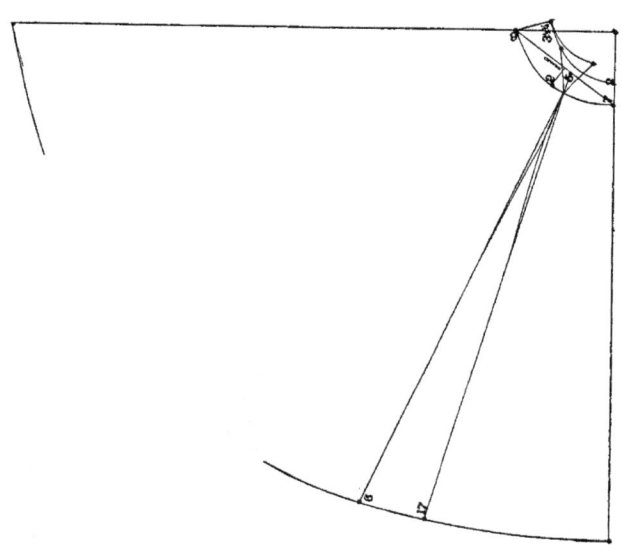

## DIAGRAM No. 39.

Empire Skirt.  עמפייר סקוירט.

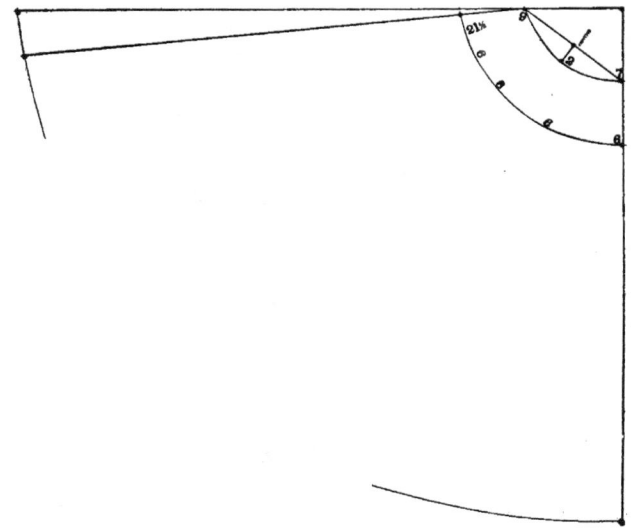

## DIAGRAM No. 40.

Circle Skirt.  סוירקעל סקוירט

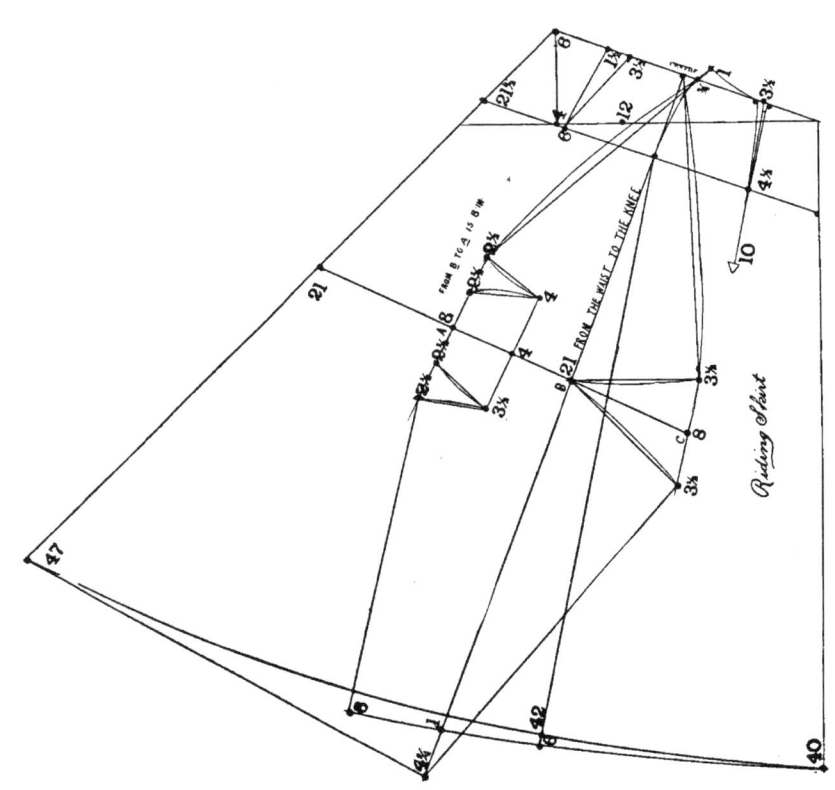

## DIAGRAM No. 41.

Riding Skirt.                רײדינג סקווירט.

### MEASURMENTS.

Waist,  24,         Front Length,  40,         Hips,  43,
         Side Length,  42,         Back Length,  47.

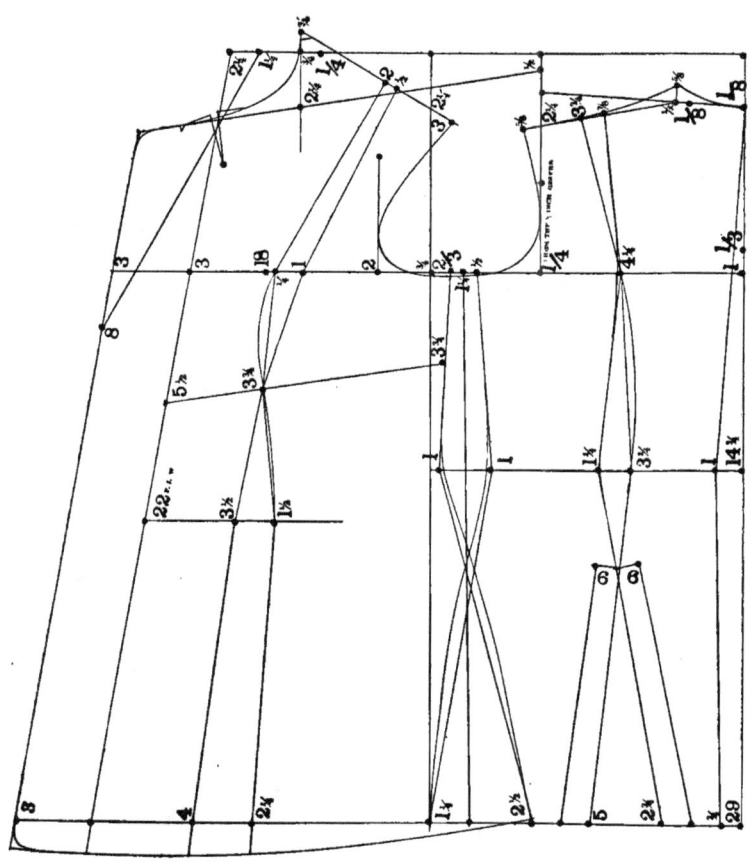

## DIAGRAM No. 42.

### Miss' Size 16.

מיסס, סייז 16

French hipless coat.   Drafted according to 34 bust.   Scale 17.

פרענטש היפלעס קאוט.   געצייכענט לויט 34 באסט.   סקעיל 17.

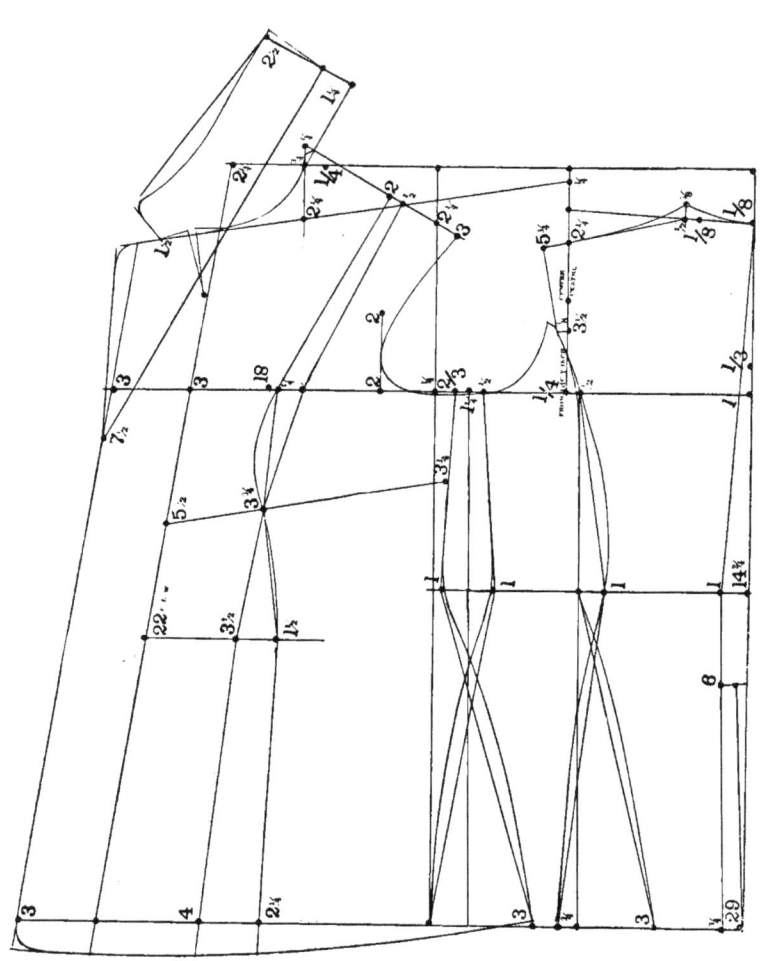

# DIAGRAM No. 43.

Miss' Size 16.   16 מיסס, סייז

French front. Drafted according to 34 bust. Scale 17.

פרענטש פראָנט. געצייכענט לויט 34 באַסט. סקעיל 17.

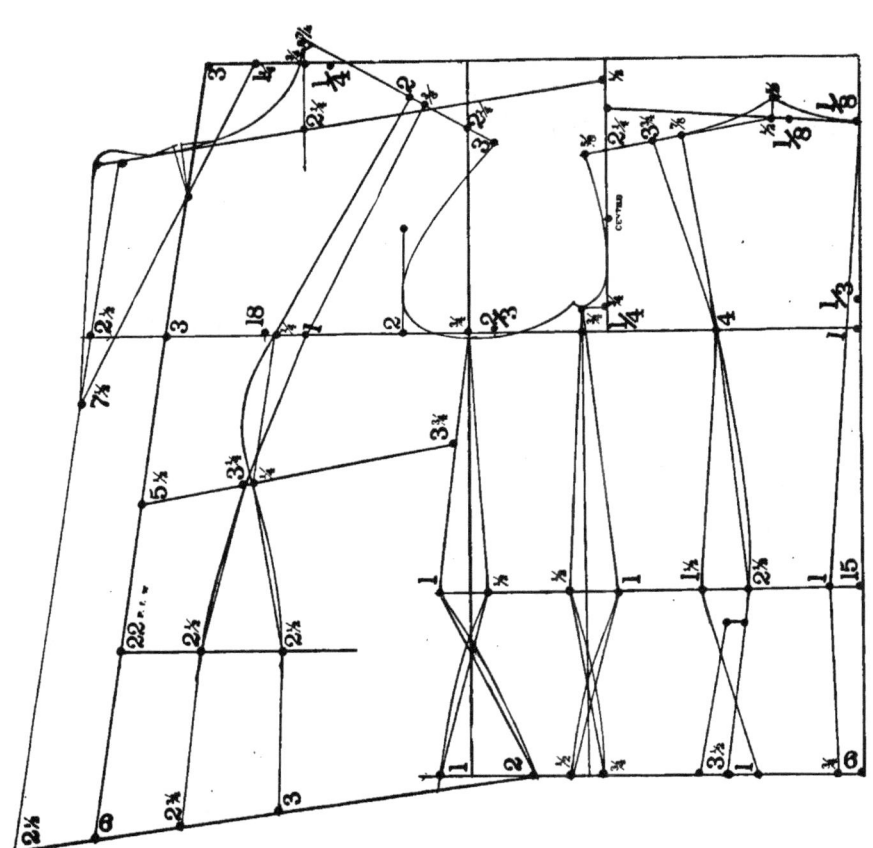

# DIAGRAM No. 44.

### Miss' tight fitting Jacket.   Size 16.

מיסס' טייט פיטטינג דזשעקעט.   סייז 16.

Drafted according to 34 bust.   Scale 17.

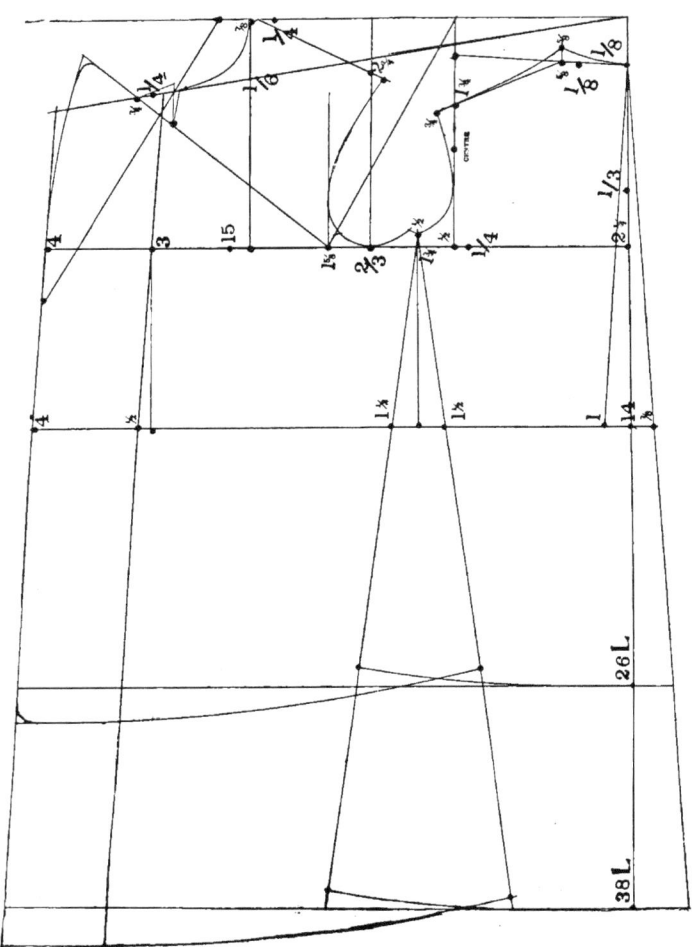

## DIAGRAM No. 45.

Box coat.    Size 8.         באקס קאוט.‏ ‏סייז 8.

Drafted according to 30 bust.    Scale 15.

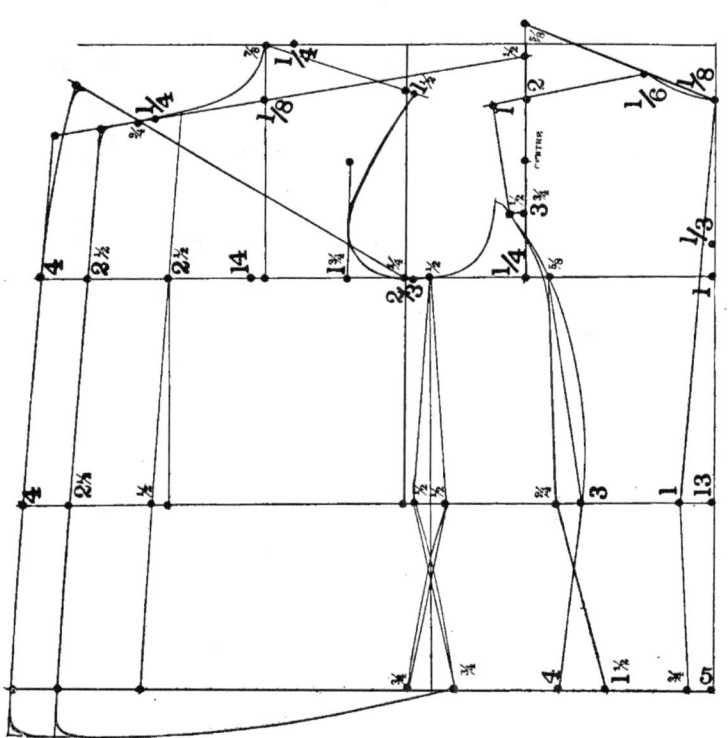

## DIAGRAM No. 46.

Children's Box Coat.   Size 8.

‫8. טשילדרענס באקס קאוט.   סײז‬

Drafted according to 28 bust.   Scale 14:

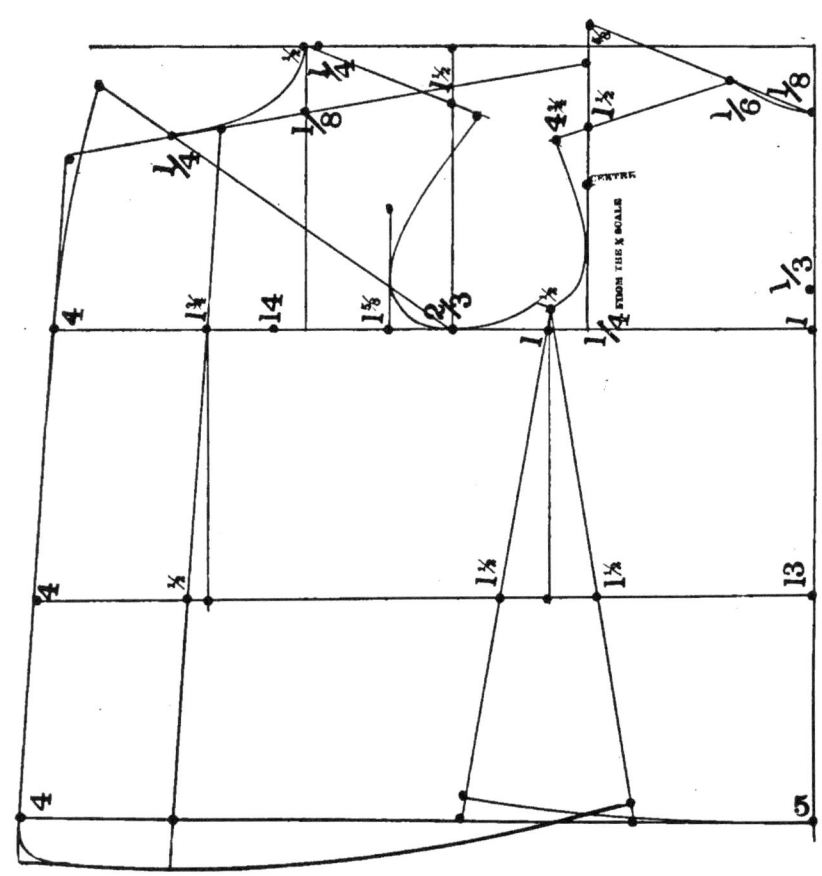

## DIAGRAM No. 47.

### Children's box coat.    Size 8.

טשילדרענס באקס קאוט.    סייז 8.

Drafted according to 28 bust.    Scale 14.

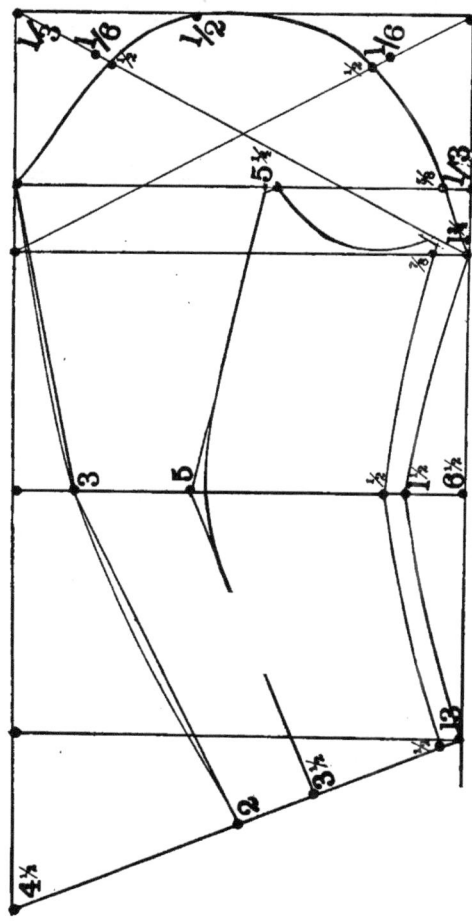

**DIAGRAM No. 48.**

Children's Sleeve.   Size 8.

טשילדרענס סליוו.   סייז 8.

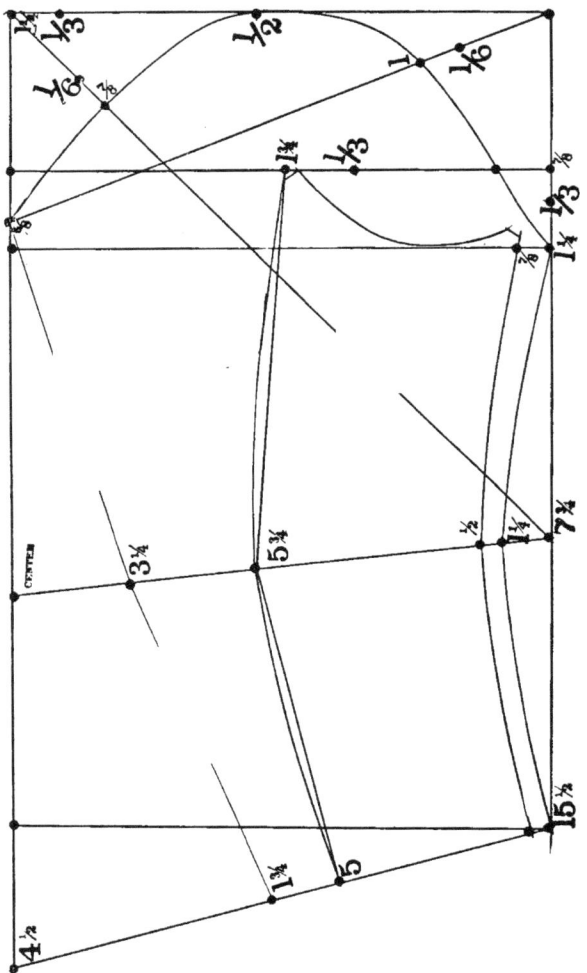

## DIAGRAM No. 49.

### Children's Sleeve.   Size 12.

טשילדרענס סליוו.  סייז 12.

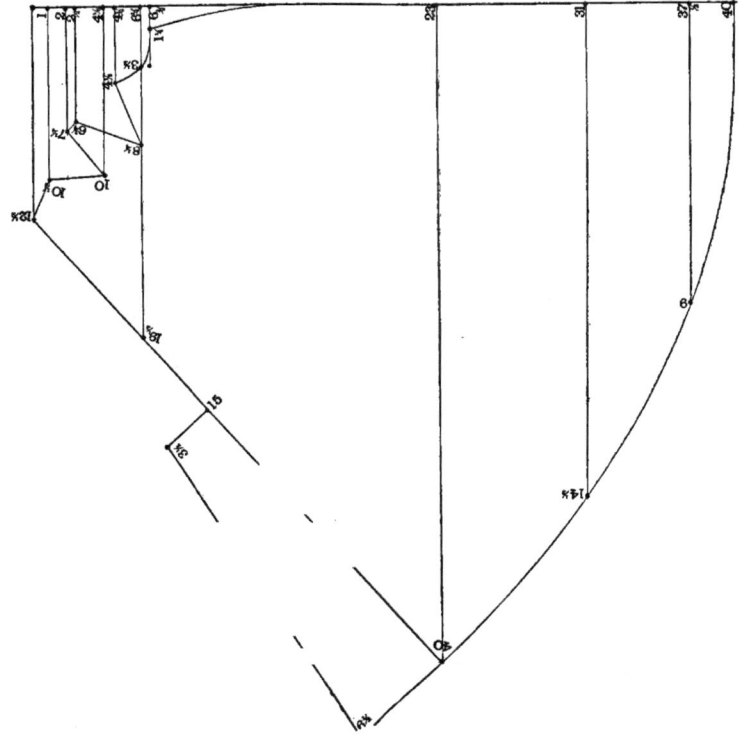

**DIAGRAM No. 50.**

Opera Coat. .אָפּערא קאָט

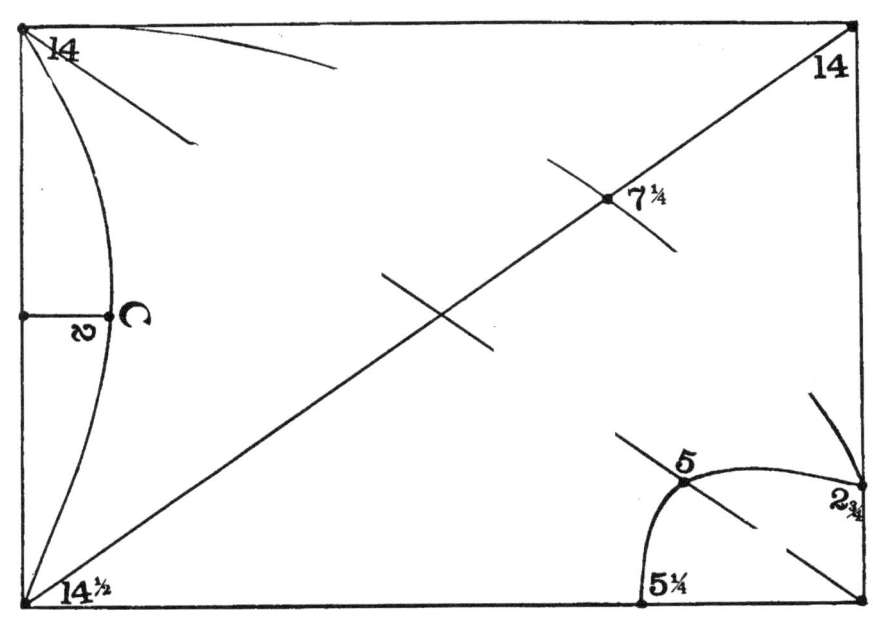

### DIAGRAM No. 51.

Hood.         הוד.

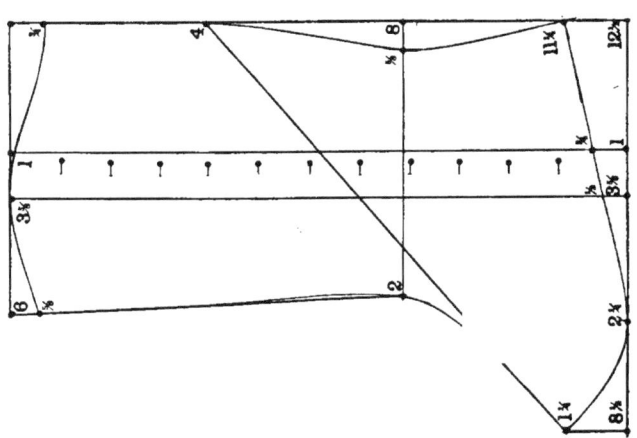

### DIAGRAM No. 52.

Legging.         לעגגינג.

# MEASUREMENTS
— OF —
## REGULAR PROPORTION.

### LADIES AND MISSES

| Age | Bust | Waist | Hips | Length Waist | Sleeve | Cuff |
|---|---|---|---|---|---|---|
| 12 | 30 | 22 | 40 | 14 | 17 | 12 |
| 14 | 32 | 23 | 41 | 14½ | 17½ | 12½ |
| 16 | 34 | 24 | 42 | 15 | 17½ | 13 |
| 18 | 36 | 25 | 43 | 15½ | 18 | 13¼ |
| 20 | 38 | 26 | 44 | 15½ | 18 | 13½ |

### CHILDREN'S AND INFANTS

| 2 | 22 | 22 | 24 | 9 | 9 | 9½ |
|---|---|---|---|---|---|---|
| 4 | 23½ | 23 | 26 | 10 | 10 | 10 |
| 6 | 25 | 24 | 28 | 11 | 11 | 10½ |
| 8 | 26½ | 25 | 30 | 12 | 12 | 11 |
| 10 | 28 | 26 | 32 | 13 | 13 | 11½ |
| 12 | 29 | 26½ | 34 | 14 | 14 | 12 |

### LADIES' SKIRTS

| Waist | Hips | Front | Side | Back |
|---|---|---|---|---|
| 25 | 43 | 42 | 43 | 44 |
| 26 | 44 | 42 | 43 | 44 |
| 28 | 45 | 42 | 43 | 44 |
| 30 | 46 | 42 | 43 | 44 |
| 32 | 48 | 42 | 43 | 44 |

### MISSES' SKIRTS

| 24 | 43 | 40 | 41 | 42 |
|---|---|---|---|---|
| 23 | 42 | 40 | 41 | 42 |
| 22 | 41 | 40 | 41 | 42 |
| 21 | 40 | 40 | 41 | 42 |
| 20 | 39 | 40 | 41 | 42 |

# INDEX.